THE AESTHETICS
OF POWER

Claire Keyes

THE AESTHETICS OF POWER: THE POETRY OF ADRIENNE RICH

THE UNIVERSITY OF GEORGIA PRESS: ATHENS AND LONDON

© 1986 by the University of Georgia Press
Athens, Georgia 30602
All rights reserved
Designed by Frank O. Williams
Set in 11 on 13 point Sabon
The paper in this book meets the guidelines for permanence and du-
rability of the Committee on Production Guidelines for Book Longev-
ity of the Council on Library Resources.

Printed in the United States of America
89 88 87 86   4 3 2 1

Library of Congress Cataloging in Publication Data

Keyes, Claire.
    The aesthetics of power.
    Bibliography: p.
    Includes index.
    1. Rich, Adrienne Cecile—Criticism and interpretations.
2. Politics in literature. 3. Feminism in literature.
I. Title.
PS3535.I233Z73 1986   811'.54   85-5866
ISBN 0-8203-0803-X (alk. paper)

The author and publisher are grateful to Adrienne Rich and W. W.
Norton & Company, Inc., for permission to quote from the following
published collections:

    Poems, Selected and New, 1950–1974, by Adrienne Rich,
    by permission of W. W. Norton & Company, Inc.
    Copyright © 1975, 1973, 1971, 1969, 1966 by W. W. Nor-
    ton & Company, Inc. Copyright © 1967, 1963, 1962,
    1961, 1960, 1959, 1958, 1957, 1956, 1955, 1954, 1953,
    1952, 1951 by Adrienne Rich.

    The Fact of a Doorframe, by Adrienne Rich, by permission
    of W. W. Norton & Company, Inc. Copyright © 1984 by
    Adrienne Rich. Copyright © 1975, 1978 by W. W. Norton
    & Company, Inc. Copyright © 1981 by Adrienne Rich.

Photograph of Adrienne Rich copyright © 1978 by Susan
Wilson. Used with permission from W. W. Norton & Company, Inc.

FOR NAN, MY MOTHER

CONTENTS

PREFACE

MANY PEOPLE have helped me in this work. Foremost among them is David Porter, and I thank him for his continuous encouragement over a long period of time. Arlyn Diamond and Lee Edwards of the University of Massachusetts guided me to the understandings I have about feminist literary criticism. I am extremely grateful, as well, to my colleague at Salem State College, Frank Devlin, upon whom I have depended for his skills as an editor. The librarians at Salem State College have made my research easier and I thank especially Elizabeth Dole and Camilla Glynn. During a residency at the Wurlitzer Foundation in Taos, New Mexico, I rewrote portions of this text and I thank Henry Sauerwein for giving me the place and the solitude to write. For their active encouragement, I thank Patricia Parker, Elizabeth Malloy, Jackie Crews, Lorraine Fine, Donna Lee Rubin, and Robin Becker. This project would never have begun had it not been for the impetus of the women's movement, and I have derived support from all my sisters—those I know and those I know only as we are working toward a common goal.

EDITIONS CITED

POETRY

A Change of World. New Haven: Yale University Press, 1951.

The Diamond Cutters and Other Poems. New York: Harper and Brothers, 1955.

Snapshots of a Daughter-in-Law: Poems, 1954–1962. New York: Harper and Row, 1963.

Necessities of Life: Poems, 1962–1965. New York: W. W. Norton, 1966.

Leaflets: Poems, 1965–1968. New York: W. W. Norton, 1969.

The Will to Change: Poems, 1968–1970. New York: W. W. Norton, 1971.

Diving into the Wreck: Poems, 1971–1972. New York: W. W. Norton, 1973.

The Dream of a Common Language: Poems, 1974–1977. New York: W. W. Norton, 1978.

A Wild Patience Has Taken Me This Far: Poems, 1978–1981. New York: W. W. Norton, 1981.

Sources. Woodside, California: Heyeck Press, 1983.

PROSE

Of Woman Born: Motherhood as Experience and Institution. New York: W. W. Norton, 1976.

On Lies, Secrets, and Silence: Selected Prose, 1966–1978. New York: W. W. Norton, 1979.

THE AESTHETICS
OF POWER

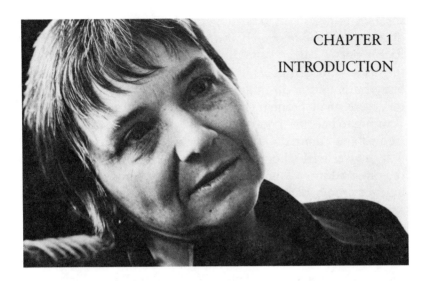

CHAPTER 1

INTRODUCTION

THOSE WHO REGARD the women's movement as the key to social and political change in our century recognize the significant role played by the poetry, prose, and person of Adrienne Rich. Her identity forged primarily through a body of remarkable poetry, Rich has become a "pioneer, witness and prophet" for the women's movement.[1] In a creative life extending from 1951 to the present, Rich has "pioneered" in the content of her poems, in her themes, and in the female aesthetic she has developed—a natural outcome of her feminist sensibility. At the core of Rich's aesthetic is an awareness of power and its constructs in the patriarchy; thus we can speak of an aesthetics of power that informs the full range of her creative output.

A brief survey of Rich's life will help clarify the elements that shaped her career and gave rise to a distinctly female aesthetics of power. Born in Maryland in 1929, the daughter of a Jewish father and a gentile mother, Rich describes herself as being "raised as a son, taught to study but not to pray, taught to hold reading and writing sacred."[2] Her father, a doctor, greatly influenced her intellectual development, and Rich's poetry is characterized by her acute intelligence and breadth of knowledge. When she was a senior at Radcliffe in 1951, Rich was selected as

the Yale Younger Poet. The judge, W. H. Auden, wrote the introduction to *A Change of World*, her first book of poems. Thus
Rich's poetic career was christened by one of the most dis-
tinguished modern poets of the twentieth century, someone she
herself admired and imitated. In addition, Rich's earliest mentors were men. From them, she learned how to write poems.
Wanting to become a poet, naturally she wrote like the poets she
studied and admired—Yeats, Auden, Stevens, Frost. This meant
that she was well schooled in the poetic craft. It also meant that
she often adopted a male persona in her poems or employed a
tone of ironic detachment, strategies that denied her womanhood. Her experience as a woman would ultimately forge an
aesthetics of power that these early poems reveal only covertly
under the surface of the traditional forms she employed.

After this early success and her graduation from Radcliffe,
Rich was awarded a Guggenheim Fellowship, traveled in Europe
and England, and married Alfred H. Conrad, an economist who
taught at Harvard. The birth of their three sons occurred during
the years she was writing the poems for *The Diamond Cutters*,
her second book. Woman of letters, wife, and mother, Rich piled
success upon success, both personally and professionally. Of
course, there were stresses; her poems reveal them. In effect, her
attention to those stresses gave birth to Rich as a woman poet.
Later, Rich documented her struggle to combine the traditional
female roles with her career as a poet in *Of Woman Born*
(1976), a study of motherhood as experience and institution.

Despite the demands of her family, she produced several more
books of poetry and won many awards. In the mid-sixties, she
lived and worked in New York City, where she became involved
in antiwar protests. At the same time, Rich read widely in wom-
en's literature and history and was drawn into a leadership role
in the women's movement through her teaching, her poetry
readings, and lectures. Thus feminism assumed a central place in
her life. An eloquent, if sometimes polemical prose writer, she
has collected the essays and reviews that she wrote during this
period (1966–79) in *On Lies, Secrets and Silence*. Its contents
range from reviews of women writers Anne Bradstreet, Char-

lotte Brontë, and Emily Dickinson to a passionate plea for "Taking Women Students Seriously." In every instance, Rich's theme is woman in the kingdom of the fathers.

Her husband committed suicide in 1970. The reasons for this remain unclear, and only indirectly through the metaphorical language of a couple of poems ("Trying to Talk with a Man" and "From a Survivor") can her readers begin to understand his death and its consequences for Rich. Otherwise, Alfred Conrad's suicide is not a subject that the poet has discussed publicly. Only in 1981–82 does she write to him as if he could hear: "I've had a sense of protecting your existence, not using it as a theme for poetry or tragic musings" (*Sources*, p. 32) Rich's delicacy and tact in this matter can only earn our respect. Her freedom from her marriage, however tragic the circumstances, seems to have liberated her sensibility, and her poems take on an angry feminist tone.

At the beginning of the seventies, Rich identified herself as a radical feminist and a lesbian separatist. In 1974, *Diving into the Wreck*, an explicitly feminist volume of poems, won the National Book Award. Rich accepted this award with two other nominees, Audre Lorde and Alice Walker, "in the name of all women." Since 1974, she has published several books of poetry and remains a feminist activist and an outspoken critic of racism.

Clearly, Adrienne Rich's influence extends from the realm of poetry to that of politics. She views the patriarchal structure of society as the root of oppression and has adopted women's issues as her primary concern, not in a narrow sense, but with the broadest possible implications for the quality of life on our endangered planet. As Nancy Milford asks in a review of *A Wild Patience Has Taken Me This Far* (1981), "What are we to do with her abundant politics before which most of us, female and male, are found lacking? We are to attend her."[3]

If we attend Adrienne Rich, she will inevitably challenge our notions of power, the central concern of this study and the concept that lies at the root of her aesthetic. The poet, like any artist, possesses creative power. As Rich's poetry shows, a woman's experience of power in the creative sphere renders her powerlessness in other areas more perplexing and problematic. The artist's ability to shape her forms does not necessarily translate to her ability to shape her environment or gain control over her life. Resolving this dilemma has occupied the poetic consciousness of Adrienne Rich for more than three decades. For her, being a woman and a poet brings into conflict the states of power and powerlessness, forcing new definitions of power, new possibilities for women, and profound repercussions for society. In her poetry, we can see the process by which Adrienne Rich embraces, then rejects accepted uses of power. Subsequently, she envisions a beneficent female power—both personal and political—predicated upon her own experience as woman and poet.

When we say, "She is a powerful poet," we imply both the poet's effect on her audience and on poetry itself. An influence has been felt. In this context, power is an "influence-term" in which "one is powerful with respect to something."[4] Adrienne Rich's poetry can certainly sustain the application of this definition of power, but the term *power* takes on more significant implications in her poetry. In *Powers of the Weak*, Elizabeth Janeway helps us understand these implications. Janeway prefers to think of power as a process and takes as epigraph to her opening chapter the statement by Karl Marx that "great social changes are impossible without the feminine ferment. Social progress can be measured exactly by the social position of the fair sex (the ugly ones included)." The curious but telling parenthetical phrase is Marx's. One imagines, to be kind, that he did not want readers to think he was considering only the beautiful courtesan or the attractive but obtuse aristocrat. Janeway notes both Marx's perception about the shifting nature of power and his emphasis on women:

> Is [power] a quality at all? or is it, rather a process that both reflects and produces "great social changes" in a continuing dynamic of human interaction? If so, it is driven by "ferments" which boil up in unexpected places while guardians of the superstructure are looking in another direction. Its "being" is "becoming." Its steady existence derives from ceaseless shifts in tensions,

its balance is maintained by thrust and response, hope and frustration, and by the practical actions that grow out of confrontations and compromises among its myriad components. . . . Marx's comment suggests that the shifts in power that are an inevitable part of change can be studied by means of "the social position of the fair sex (the ugly ones included."[5]

To Janeway, as to Marx, power can be better understood as a process and not simply a quality. To observe that process, she advocates a focus upon women and their "social position." Given Adrienne Rich's status as a poet, her central concern with women's issues, and her emphasis upon power, the body of her work provides an observable world in microcosm where power as a process can be studied. Furthermore, what Marx terms "feminine ferment" constitutes a key aspect of that process, if we interpret this phrase as signifying woman's crucial role in the transformation of society. Adrienne Rich shares with Marx and Janeway a concern with the position of women in the patriarchy and with the dynamics of change.

In patriarchal systems, power in public forms is taboo for women, and only the extraordinary woman breaks through what Dorothy Dinnerstein calls "the male monopoly of formal, overt power."[6] Adrienne Rich confirms this assessment when she quotes from "A Pastoral Letter from the Congregational Church," the reprimand to the Grimke sisters (and other women): "The power of woman is her dependence, flowing from the consciousness of that weakness which God has given her for her protection. But when she assumes the place and tone of man as a public reformer . . . she yields the power which God has given her for her protection, and her character becomes unnatural."[7] Such a definition of woman's power relegates her to perpetual subjugation and denies the trend of modern history, at least in developed nations. In her poetry, Adrienne Rich gradually forges a new definition of woman's power. Her progression toward its full articulation and advocacy began with intimations of ideas in her earliest work.

In her first book of poems, *A Change of World* (1951), the twenty-one-year-old Adrienne Rich accepts certain traditions associated with the division of power according to sex. In these same poems, however, we detect subversive undercurrents and an assertion of power whenever her persona combines artistry with womanhood. These assertions appear mainly unconscious although utterly in keeping with a body of myths about the relationship of women to art. Rich, the Radcliffe senior who wrote these poems, was most likely aware of Greek myths where female divinities govern the arts, from dance to music to poetry. Female power in the arts did not, however, translate to power in any political context.[8] Adrienne Rich's poetry points the way toward how such a translation might occur. In three decades of poetry, up to *The Dream of a Common Language* (1978) and *A Wild Patience Has Taken Me This Far* (1981), Rich continually defines and redefines her concept of power until she can reject power-as-force (patriarchal power) for the power-to-transform, which, for her, is "the truly significant and essential power," one she comes to understand because of her womanhood.[9]

The relationship between womanhood and transforming power extends back to the connection made from prehistoric times onward between woman and nature: the Earth perceived as a woman, the Great Goddess, Magna Mater, Mother Nature.[10] In Adrienne Rich's claiming of such power as intrinsic to woman, she calls for a "return to the root: *posse, potere, pouvoir*—to be able, to have the potential, to possess and use one's energy of creation: transforming power."[11] As an artist, Rich has cultivated this transforming power;[12] as a woman cut off from "formal, overt power" and deeply critical of its uses, she has searched for and located a viable alternative. Not the "misering of resources," such power, for her, becomes "the drive to connect / the dream of a common language." As this study will show, her notions of power shape the content and forms of her poems.

First, some basic assumptions: power as *control* is acquired through intelligence, will, and action—sometimes violent. Such power is bad or good according to its use. Through most of recorded history man has held political and social control and woman has achieved her status or "mystique" because man granted it to her. Man has experienced himself as agent and woman has been relegated to the position of Other—even to herself.

The most profound analysis of woman as Other, and therefore without overt power, comes from Simone de Beauvoir's landmark study *The Second Sex,* published in France in 1949. She regards woman's subservient role as originating during the Bronze Age, when man became a worker with tools:

> Man learns his power. In the relation of his creative arm to the fabricated object he experiences causation: planted grain may or may not germinate, but metal always reacts in the same way to fire, to tempering, to mechanical treatment. This world of tools could be embraced within clear concepts: rational thought, logic, and mathematics could now appear. The whole concept of the universe is overthrown. The religion of woman was bound to the region of irreducible duration, of contingency, of chance, of waiting, of mystery; the reign of Homo faber is the reign of time manageable as space, of necessary consequences, of the project, of action, or reason. . . . From then on, it was to be the male principle of creative force, of light, of intelligence, of order, that he would recognize as sovereign. . . . Condemned to play the part of the Other, woman was also condemned to hold only uncertain power: slave or idol, it was never she who chose her lot.[13]

In Simone de Beauvoir's construct, the division between man and woman becomes a division of different kinds of power. Man develops his power through logos—"the male principle of creative force, of light, of intelligence, of order." Woman's "uncertain" power remains in the other realm—of dark instead of light, of chance instead of control, of the unconscious. De Beauvoir's way of seeing the separation of powers is congruent with Freud's and Jung's. Her emphasis, however, is upon woman. As a feminist, de Beauvoir maintains that woman will remain in her position as Other until she, like man, learns her power. At that point, theoretically, outmoded power constructs will dissolve. In this same vein of feminist thought we can locate Adrienne Rich.

As a feminist poet, Adrienne Rich develops a female aesthetic, a woman's art shaped by the power-to-transform.[14] Of course, a woman can be a poet without being a feminist. Many have done so. In this respect, Barbara and Albert Gelpi contrast H.D. (Hilda Doolittle) with Adrienne Rich, saying that "although [H.D.'s] imagination was responding in large part to the political and social upheavals of [World War II and the cold war,] her response was characteristically 'womanly': she did not engage the political realities directly . . . but withdrew further and further inward to celebrate the psychological and mystical dimensions of woman's mysteries."[15] Adrienne Rich, however, does not withdraw; her intent is to "reconstitute the world," as she says in her poem "Natural Resources" (1977).

In this respect, Adrienne Rich is part of what she herself terms "a movement of the human psyche: a seeming cultural rejection of masculinism itself." She joins notable women thinkers such as Simone de Beauvoir, Karen Horney, and M. Esther Harding.[16] While identifying the rejection of masculinism in male writers Denis de Rougemont and Erich Neumann,[17] Rich is concerned with the ultimate direction of their thinking. By the mid-fifties, she writes, both of them "had begun to identify the denial of 'the feminine' in civilization with the roots of inhumanity and self-destructiveness and to call for a renewal of 'the feminine principle'" ("The Kingdom of the Fathers," p. 29). She regards such a return to the "feminine" in their work as something "elusive and abstract . . . , [having] little connection with the rising expectations and consciousness of actual women" (p. 30).

Rich's comment on de Rougemont and Neumann and the limitation imposed by their maleness is characteristic of her later development as a radical lesbian feminist. She is obsessed by women—their centuries-old oppression, their liberation. This obsession charges her poetry and prose with its single-minded focus; it also blinds her to the value of any non-female expression, however well intentioned or accurate. In rejecting masculinism, she rejects men. She underplays this rejection and considers any questioning of her separatist position as wrongheaded. "The point," she says, in arguing for "new words . . . written by women entirely to and for women, . . . is not the 'exclusion' of men; it is that primary presence of women to ourselves and each other first described by Mary Daly, and which is the crucible of a new language" (*On Lies, Secrets, and Silence*, p. 249). Rich's dream of a new language capable of transforming the world is magnificent; of such dreams are great poets made. Nonetheless, her readers must recognize where Rich's obsessiveness becomes dogmatic, detracting from the truth of her position and the beauty of its poetic forms.

Adrienne Rich's intent in developing a female aesthetic coincides with the goals of the women's movement. As she points out, "Truly to liberate women, then, means to change thinking itself: finally to reintegrate what has been named the unconscious, the subjective, the emotional with the structural, the rational, the intellectual, to 'connect the prose and the passion' in [E. M.] Forster's phrase; and finally to annihilate those dichotomies" ("The Kingdom of the Fathers," p. 34). While giving credit to the male novelist, Rich's concept is concerned with the new being of women. Furthermore, as Helen Vendler so aptly comments, Rich's single-minded focus calls into question her knowledge of similar movements and of contributions made by men.

> The concept—that an inclusive consciousness is to be preferred to a disembodied or repressed one—is one endorsed in every century anew, and found too painful by most inhabitants of every century except for the greatest artists. But Rich's language ignores the honorable history of this idea, and espouses inclusiveness as a "new form of thinking" to be practiced by women, who will thereby free themselves from the death-culture of abstraction and quantification. Why not tell women to imitate Keats or Shakespeare? There are models for such "thinking through the body"; that they are men does not vitiate their usefulness.[18]

Helen Vendler makes a good point; any reasonable person would have to agree with her and balk at Rich's insistence on denying the "usefulness" of male artists and thinkers. Yet Rich, in her own way, makes remarkable sense: the "superior" position of the male—artist or otherwise—has blocked the female; women have not harnessed their own power. Women, up to the very recent past, have not identified the sources of their power.

Discover that power through language, Rich says, womanly language. Writing to and for women—and excluding men—is a radical experiment in forging a new consciousness.

In effect, Adrienne Rich's purpose is to create "a new kind of human being," one who is outside the traditions shaped by patriarchal culture. Thus a study that focuses upon the theme of power in her poetry takes us beyond de Rougemont and Neumann in the history of consciousness and into the configurations of what Rich calls a "post-androgynous" society ("The Kingdom of the Fathers," p. 35). This vision, propelled by her evolution of a female aesthetic, also raises questions about what this special focus upon power implies for the development of women's poetry.

As a poet, Adrienne Rich makes certain choices regarding diction, syntax, imagery, musical values, and prosody—that is, the components of poetic form. Governing these choices is her womanhood. Among the motifs that emerge as central to her aesthetic are: an emphasis on woman's silence, the transformation of which will mark a shift in power relationships; a woman-centered poetic tradition that validates woman's art, women artists, and other women; an acknowledgment of the female principle as the locus of transforming power; and the designation of woman's body as metaphor of the life-force itself with "the passion to make and make again where such unmaking reigns" (as she writes in her poem "Natural Resources"). Therefore, Rich's sex is at the root of her aesthetic. She may avoid this fact unconsciously or consciously; she may fight it, deny it, or accept it, but her poems come from a female imagination and that imagination can be glimpsed wherever the issue of power surfaces.[19]

To be a poet is to have power, not only in the creation of new forms, but in the effects that those new forms have upon the human psyche. Most would agree that the power of poetry is not executive, but educative and spiritual. Thus Carl Jung describes the use of poetry and all the arts: the long-range goal of art is "to educate the spirit of the age, bringing to birth those forms in which the age is most lacking."[20] This is no small claim. In a recent essay, Terrence Des Pres reminds us that the "ultimate concern" of our age is the threat of nuclear annihiliation. To what power can poetry aspire against the destruction of a thousand Hiroshimas? Des Pres states, "We turn to words which give the spirit breathing space and strength to endure. As in any time of ultimate concern, we call on poetry." Surveying contemporary poets, Des Pres cites Carolyn Forche and Adrienne Rich as among the few who answer this call because they do not reject "history and politics on principle" in a quest for a poetry of the self.[21]

In becoming a political poet, Rich ultimately separates herself from an American poetic represented by T. S. Eliot, Wallace Stevens, and Robert Frost and rooted in the thought and practice of Ralph Waldo Emerson. As a transcendental idealist, Emerson perceived the poet, the representative man, as one deeply connected to the natural world, which yielded its meanings to him. Thus he could say, "Every natural fact is a symbol of some spiritual fact." For Emerson, nature became a source of images necessary for the development of the self; politics was a distraction from the self's higher urgencies. He refused to become involved in the abstract cause of abolition or to help the faraway poor when asked to contribute to a fund. He was not heartless: he would give to the poor in *his* town. No social reformer, he distrusted causes and movements, anything that smacked of the "mob." Because of his influence, the celebration of "the self as a world" rather than "the self in the world" became the prime focus of poetic activity in America, even to this day.[22] In Terrence Des Pres's estimation, "Our poets in the main have been satisfied to stick with Emerson, and few would find anything to take exception with in the following lines from Emerson's 'Ode' ":[23]

> I cannot leave
> My honied thought
> For the priest's cant,
> Or the statesman's rant.
>
> If I refuse
> My study for their politique,

Which at the best is trick,
The angry Muse
Puts confusion in my brain.

Emerson influenced many American poets and thus a tradition arose in which "the trick" of politics did not enter poetry though it might enter other writings by the same poets who eschewed it.[24] Influenced by this tradition, and schooled by the formalism of the new criticism to value T. S. Eliot rather than William Carlos Williams, Wallace Stevens and Robert Frost over Ezra Pound and Charles Olson, Rich did not emerge as a political poet until the mid-sixties.[25] At this point, she risked the "confusion" Emerson feared.

The seeds of this development can be detected in her early work, and more precisely in the area of women and power. Rich stands out in her call for men and women to recognize the value not just of the feminine principle, but of individual women and their lives—what's "most lacking" to her in our age. Such a call would reverse the strengthening of masculine consciousness and challenge those unquestioned assumptions that lead "not only to the continuing destruction of women, but to the murder of the planet."[26] Thus her poems become part of one of the great movements of the twentieth century. In such a context, the poet has power.

At times, according to the prevailing taste in contemporary poetry, Adrienne Rich ventures into territory considered off limits to lyrical poetry, becoming, some critics assert, less of a poet, even less "womanly" in her concern for issues larger than the individual human heart. As this study will show, Rich stretches the boundaries of what is considered "good"—whether in poetry or in the concerns of women. In "attending" her, as Nancy Milford says we must, we are doing something relatively new in the history of literature. Most poets are men writing in a masculine tradition. That is, they think through men poets and their freedom as creative beings is based upon their status in a culture, literary and otherwise, that validates human experience as male experience. On this point, Simone de Beauvoir writes:

Art, literature, philosophy, are attempts to found the world anew on a human liberty: that of the individual creator; to entertain such a pretension, one must first unequivocally assume the status of a being who has liberty. The restrictions that education and custom impose on woman now limit her grasp on the universe; when that struggle to find one's place in this world is too arduous, there can be no question of getting away from it. Now, one must first emerge from it into a sovereign solitude if one wants to re-gain a grasp upon it: what woman needs first of all is to under-take, in anguish and pride, her apprenticeship in abandonment and transcendence: that is, in liberty. (*The Second Sex*, p. 669)

In the mid-twentieth century, when Adrienne Rich first started publishing her poetry, that grasp upon the universe and the free-dom to abandon it were masculine prerogatives. Things have changed, and feminist writing since the late sixties has both commented upon and contributed to those changes in women's status. This new focus on the being and becoming of woman— her history, her concerns, her art—records a shift in our atten-tion and an expansion of consciousness.

My book builds upon the feminist criticism that came out of the women's movement of the late sixties. The historical events of that decade, from civil rights demonstrations to antiwar pro-tests, created a climate of opposition that was the chief emo-tional drive of the women's movement and of women's poetry at the time. As Louise Bernikow points out in a retrospective arti-cle on women's poetry, "It is particularly appropriate that poetry emerge as the art form of that political moment. There were political meetings preceded by poetry readings. . . . This feeding of literary talent by an essentially political source is not new in the history of the world, but what it has done for women in our time . . . is restore the art of poetry to a primitive, tribal function."[27] As the lists of poets grew—Bernikow mentions many, including Adrienne Rich, June Jordan, Anne Sexton, Joan Larkin, Alice Walker, Erica Jong, Denise Levertov, Nikki Giovanni, Audre Lorde—women in the academy began "to at-tend to the contemporaries." Feminist literary criticism takes its impulse from the great surge in women's literature and also from the same desire to seek out, as Bernikow says of women's poetry, "Lines of descent and heritage . . . , the search and construction of a female past."[28]

Feminist literary criticism assumes the value of a focus upon women's art as a legitimate and essential field of inquiry. This is particularly true of the work of Adrienne Rich, both prose and poetry, for she takes as her aim the attempt "to found the world anew" on the liberation of women. She is, of course, only one of many women, poets and nonpoets, engaged in this project. Because of the impressive body of her work and the themes and issues that she handles, she and her poetry demand special attention.

An examination of Adrienne Rich's poetry and prose from 1951 to the present indicates the difficult process by which she moves toward a new understanding of the power of the poet and the power of women. Naturally, the political and social climate of post–World War II America conditioned her process. The cultural revolution of the sixties and the turmoil surrounding the Vietnam War affected the woman whom the reviewer Ellen Moers deems "one of America's most important and gifted poets."[29] An awareness of these influences can tell us as much about out institutions as about the poet. In effect, Adrienne Rich's poetry constitutes an indictment of the times, specifically those power structures that limit and dehumanize us all.

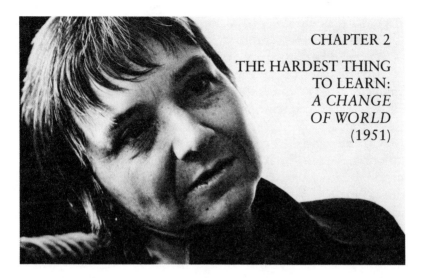

CHAPTER 2

THE HARDEST THING
TO LEARN:
*A CHANGE
OF WORLD*
(1951)

READING THE EARLY POEMS of Adrienne Rich and looking for the feminist visionary of her later poems can be an acute disappointment. Or it can be an exercise in the new feminist criticism that looks for what Elaine Showalter calls "a double-voiced discourse containing a 'dominant' and a 'muted' story."[1] For most women writers up to the recent past, that dominant story coincides with mainstream patriarchal values, where power, for example, is a male prerogative and subservience the prevailing mode of female behavior. The muted story follows a different course; in it can be heard "maternal precursors," to use Showalter's phrase.

Although Showalter analyzes plots in women's fiction, her concept can also be applied to poetry. In detecting this double-voiced discourse in literature by women, the reader confronts an "object/field problem" in which the dominant story and the muted story alternate as different possibilities for interpreting the text: Is it a vase that you see or a face? Once you have seen the face, you no longer regard the vase conventionally and vice versa. The "plots" of Rich's early poems may present an orthodox "vase," but the muted story emerges as the true "face" of the poet. Adrrienne Rich's muted story, as we shall see, contains the seeds of her feminist vision.

Elizabeth Abel, the editor of *Writing and Sexual Difference* in which Showalter's essay appears, alerts her readers that "Female characters and female authors alike emerge as ingenious strategists who succeed in devising some mode of assertion." Women writers are "resilient," says Abel, and make their assertions in resourceful ways. She cites George Eliot's *The Mill on the Floss* and argues that "Even Maggie Tulliver, an obvious exception, here dies in the service of her author's self-discovery, not as victim of society." Abel points to other "unlikely" heroes in her collection: Helen of Troy, Petrarch's Laura, and Freud's Dora. "The critical focus on sexual difference," Abel says, "may increase our recognition of unorthodox female creative strategies" in women characters and women writers (*Writing and Sexual Difference*, p. 6). The youthful Adrienne Rich emerges as an "ingenious strategist," with her womanhood in a male-dominated culture contributing to the double-voiced discourse in *A Change of World*.

W. H. Auden devotes half of his introduction to Rich's volume to explaining why poems written in 1951 suffer in comparison to poems written by the previous generation of poets, the great moderns. In assessing those who were "the creators of a new style," Auden says he finds himself "with a list of twenty persons. It was these *men* who were driven to find a new style which could cope with [wide-ranging] changes in our civilization" (emphasis added). It was simply the fate of a young poet like Rich to come after the innovators. Do not look for innovations in these poems; in fact, "They make no attempt to conceal their family tree"—Frost and Yeats, the poets Auden mentions.[2] In this way the poetry of Adrienne Rich was introduced to the public. She is a good imitator. Within that imitation, however, she devises "a mode of assertion" undetected by Auden and, most likely, unconscious to herself. The subtlety of this assertion contributed to the ease with which Auden accepted her into the circle of men poets, without, it seems, too much attention to her being a woman.

Granted, Auden praises Rich for traditional "feminine" virtues like dutifulness and self-restraint. He says that her poems tell the truth and that she knows her craft. Auden mostly praises her *modesty*, a term he uses twice, summing up his opinion of the volume by saying that the poems are "neatly and modestly dressed" and that they "speak quietly but do not mumble, respect their elders but are not cowed by them, and do not tell fibs." Yet these poems do contain lies, albeit unconscious, that Rich had to tell in order to win recognition. If that recognition contained condescension, if Auden might not praise a young male poet in the same terms, so be it. This was 1951, after all, and Rich was a "feminine" woman and poet.

In his praise Auden fixes Adrienne Rich in a cultural moment in midcentury America—six years after Hiroshima—when to conserve the traditions seemed more important than any radical breaking away. Exploring that moment, Betty Friedan, in her 1963 classic *The Feminine Mystique*, defined the terms and consequences of female subservience, one of the most widely accepted of modern traditions. Auden, although not a feminist, is similarly attuned to the time period when he says: "Radical changes and significant novelty in artistic style, can only occur when there has been a radical change in human sensibility to require them." After the chaos of World War II, those changes would require another decade or more to surface in civil rights, antiwar, and women's movements. Indeed, the sensibility reflected in *A Change of World* is conservative not radical, tradition-bound rather than making its own traditions, feminine rather than female. These are poems of their time and yet a comment upon their time with resonances of more complicated intentions. Those intentions have to do with women and power.

Twenty-four years after the publication of her first book Adrienne Rich writes:

> Outside of the mother's brief power over the child—subject to patriarchal interference—women have experienced power in two forms, both of them negative. The first is men's power over us—whether physical, economic, or institutional. . . . . Like other dominated people, we have learned to manipulate and seduce, or

> to internalize men's will and make it ours, and men have some-
> times characterized this as "power" in us; but it is nothing more
> than the child's or courtesan's "power" to wheedle and the depen-
> dent's "power" to disguise her feelings—even from herself—in
> order to obtain favors or, literally, to survive. . . . Women have
> also felt man's powerfulness in the root sense of the word (*potere,
> posse,* or *pouvoir*—to be able, to be capable)—expressed in the
> creations of his mind. Powerfulness is the expressive energy of an
> ego which, unlike ours, was licensed to thrust itself outward upon
> the world. ("The Kingdom of the Fathers," pp. 22–23)

When power is linked to maleness, force, or both, woman's experience of it becomes negative. In neither instance is woman the
agent. Either she is the one upon whom the power is exercised or
else she is deemed incapable of "expressive energy" because she
is not male. In many ways, Adrienne Rich's first three books of
poems—*A Change of World, The Diamond Cutters, Snapshots
of a Daughter-in-Law*—reflect woman's negative experience, the
consequences of which can be charted in Rich's double-voiced
discourse.

As Rich points out, women have developed the "courtesan's
'power' to wheedle" that most of the time involves the element of
disguise. A mask is put on in order to gain favor or position that
the woman cannot openly achieve or demand for herself. That
mask can, of course, be a certain kind of language or tone, perhaps a gentle acceptance or modesty. Flattery takes form in the
imitation of man's words or attitudes—anything that will please
or seduce. Naturally, restraint of actual feeling composes the sub-
stratum of disguise. Whereas man can express the energy of his
ego, woman must hold within in order "to survive." Such withholding is negative in that it turns against the self and prevents the
development of the woman's potential and humanity. One does
not become fully existent if restraint is the primary mode. "To
exist," Simone de Beauvoir writes, "is to cast oneself into the
world. Those who occupy themselves in restraining this original
movement can be considered as sub-men." For women, restraint
and disguise bring on, of course, envy and resentment of man's
powerfulness. Adrienne Rich's creative energies as poet offset this

18

catalog of debilities. Though her early work exhibits a negative experience of power, as a poet she gains more expressive energy with every poem she writes. Thus the chief quality in her early poetry is a tension between energy and restraint.

Rich's female personas in certain key poems accept the sense that women's energies should be checked while at the same time longing for more active expression: the ability to change sex roles and social structures that limit woman's freedom. This ambivalence in her first volume of poems is caused by equating power with virility and questioning the propriety of woman's having such a masculine trait. Clearly, *A Change of World* is by a young woman, imitating accepted social patterns and the formalism of other poets she admired. Even so, the poet demonstrates the first adult signs of her own potential as an active agent in a rapidly changing world.

In this collection, the poem "An Unsaid Word" makes a good beginning for an analysis of woman's negative experience of power. Characterized by the themes of denial, evasion, and disguise, this seven-line poem concerns a "good" woman who could get the attention of her man through her power to seduce him. She chooses not to do this, thus the "unsaid word."

> She who has power to call her man
> From that estranged intensity
> Where his mind forages alone,
> Yet keeps her peace and leaves him free,
> And when his thoughts to her return
> Stands where he left her, still his own,
> Knows this the hardest thing to learn.

If there is a double voice in this poem, the dominant one prevails. It tells the story of a woman's willing subservience to sexual roles that allow a man to wander free while a woman stands still "where he left her." In effect, the woman appears as the fulfillment of a male fantasy, for she mutes her power and remains silent, her words of desire or complaint "unsaid." Because this woman is modest and unassuming, she keeps her man. The poem is an object lesson in the sexual politics of the fifties.

The dominant voice appears in the gracefulness of the style as well, which is formal in its scansion, its rhyme scheme, its syntax and diction. The poem is beautiful in its formal elegance, its thought articulated in a syntactically perfect, single sentence that scans—but not monotonously so—its basic iambic tetrameter asserting itself most elegantly in lines 4 and 7. The fluidity of the syntax is uninterrupted by the rhyme scheme (ABABAAA), which appears effortless, graceful, and unstrained. No slang or colloquialism mars the poetic diction. One imagines the speaker as highbred, compassionate, and intelligent. She is no shrew, no common woman who might complain or turn sullen. The speaker identifies with her persona and the intimate tone of this identification makes separation between speaker and persona difficult to perceive. Entering into the persona's consciousness, the speaker knows what the woman could do but does not, what the woman desires but denies. She knows how hard it is to maintain the self-restraint necessary to keep a stable relationship with a man and she gives the woman the credit she is due.

Auden was right: the twenty-one-year-old Rich knew her craft and had learned the lessons of her masters. It seems almost vulgar in this context to insist upon the muted voice that breaks through, even though delicately, the formal elegance of this slight poem from Rich's apprenticeship. That muted voice can be detected in the relationship between the title of the poem "An Unsaid Word" and the first phrase: "She who has power." For there it is: a woman's true power, not her negative experience of power, lies in language. Instead of language using women, as the formal language of this poem uses Adrienne Rich, women must "begin to grasp [language as] a material resource that women have never before collectively attempted to repossess" (*On Lies, Secrets, and Silence*, p. 247). Those unsaid words are the woman's power; to dam back that power is "the hardest thing to learn."

The nascent, but unsure feminism in "An Unsaid Word" emerges in the ambiguous last line that gives way to an unconscious irony. Why is "this the hardest thing to learn"? And what does *this* refer to in its poetic context? Presumably the woman denies her desire for her man for the sake of his freedom. Her denial of her own needs constitutes the difficulty. This line could go another way: it is hard to learn the subterfuges demanded by a woman's role. Those subterfuges limit a woman's activity (she stands still) while granting the man the full exercise of his powers. In fact, his freedom seems predicated upon the limitations imposed on the woman. She finds these limits confining because she must repress her most elemental feelings.

Rich's ambiguity in the last line turns the poem another way by implying a criticism of sex roles that limit a woman to such negative experiences as denial and disguise. At this point, at least in her poetry, Rich could not openly allow such a thought and it remains only a suggestive possibility. Perhaps she thinks it, but does not dare say so; maybe she does not comprehend the full implications of sex roles. We can only speculate. More "knowing" than the competent, conscious poet, the irony of the last line allows the muted voice to break through the graceful, orderly surface of the poem.

Woman's sense of her own ability to create—to roam freely, to act, to be alone—pulls against all the forces willing her to be dependent: to "stand where he left her, still his own," that is, to be a traditional woman. Rich's persona does not possess her own being; she depends upon man to validate her partial existence. From this deeply ambivalent beginning, Rich's poetry moves toward the shaping of forms of female power predicated upon a woman's possession of her own soul.

While Adrienne Rich could not show overtly in her early poems the female foraging alone in her own estranged intensity, she does show veiled images of that action which could lead to an assertion of a woman's power. Two poems that present women practicing needlework, "Mathilde in Normandy" and "Aunt Jennifer's Tigers," are metaphors for the divided self, double-voiced poems in which women cannot "own" their power outright. In both of these poems, however, woman transcends the traditional dependency of her role by means of her "craft." The complex interaction between the womanly role and the role of woman as artist (thus aberrant) forms a thematic nucleus in

Rich's early poetry. This interaction leads us further into woman's negative experience of power and the ensuing forms of disguise and denial.

"Aunt Jennifer's Tigers" gives us, among other things, an image of the artist as woman. In this poem, as in "An Unsaid Word," the speaker remains outside the action and comments upon it. In contrast to the previous poem, the tone seldom approaches intimacy, the speaker seeming fairly detached from the fate of Aunt Jennifer, her persona. The dominant voice of the poem asserts the traditional theme that art outlives the person who produces it. Representing creative power, or art, the tigers in the tapestry Aunt Jennifer embroiders are the focus of the opening stanza. The final stanza indicates that they will endure while Aunt Jennifer will die and that they will continue to represent her unfulfilled longings.

> Aunt Jennifer's tigers prance across a screen,
> Bright topaz denizens of a world of green.
> They do not fear the men beneath the tree;
> They pace in sleek chivalric certainty.
>
> Aunt Jennifer's fingers fluttering through her wool
> Find even the ivory needle hard to pull.
> The massive weight of Uncle's wedding band
> Sits heavily upon Aunt Jennifer's hand.
>
> When Aunt is dead, her terrified hands will lie
> Still ringed with ordeals she was mastered by.
> The tigers in the panel that she made
> Will go on prancing, proud and unafraid.

In their strength, activity, and freedom from fear, the tigers are images of virility projected by the woman but not claimed by her as one with her being. Her success in her "craft" does not translate into personal power in life. She is portrayed as a timid victim. Rich's images of Aunt Jennifer describe parts of her—fingers and hands. We never see the whole woman until she is dead. Because she never integrates the "tigers" into her psyche, Aunt Jennifer remains ambivalent toward them. To accept the implication of being a tiger is to unwoman herself, especially since the tigers prance around in "sleek chivalric certainty"—obviously male chevaliers, "proud and unafraid." The image of Aunt Jennifer's fingers suggests another theme. "Uncle's wedding band" weighs the woman down. Rich reinforces this theme by using "ringed" in the last quatrain. Aunt Jennifer's "ordeals" stem from her marital situation; her victimhood is pitiful, her husband oppressive. Thus she experiences Uncle's power negatively—and she will die: "When Aunt is dead, her terrified hands will lie / Still ringed with ordeals she was mastered by."

The tigers live on. The speaker is almost callous in her disregard for Aunt's death as her focus returns to the beautiful tigers. It is the reader's reaction as well. We cannot help admiring the beauty of Rich's imagery and diction, the fluidity of her scansion seeming, as Randall Jarrell describes it, "close to water, close to air" (ARP, p. 127). Even her rhymes are perfect: screen/green, wool/pull. If anything is sleek, chivalric, and certain, it is Rich's control over the devices of her craft. The formal beauty of the poem is such that we would rather deny the mundane ordinariness of this woman, who could be anyone's aunt, her story is so common. Who cares that Aunt Jennifer dies? The speaker does not seem to; she gets caught up in those gorgeous tigers—those "Bright topaz denizens." Here lies the dominant voice: Aunt is not compelling; her creation is.

The muted voice asserts something different and more threatening to the concept of what is art and who may make it. The poem assumes that this ordinary woman's embroidery is art. It assumes this and builds upon it, moving into the statement of its traditional theme—life is short (and terrible); art is long (and beautiful)—so that one can hardly stop and challenge its basic premise: an ordinary woman creates a work of art in her handicraft. Does it not seem possible, then, to perceive a sly ambiguity in Rich's use and placement of the word *lie*? What will these hands lie about? That they were terrified? That the creation of the "Bright topaz denizens" stemmed naturally from a woman's hands? Rich's ambiguity in her last stanza suggests another manifestation of the muted story in the tigers themselves.

Projections of the aunt's fantasy life, the tigers assert their own confidence, freedom, and beauty independent of men: "They do not fear the men beneath the tree; / They pace in sleek chivalric certainty." The virile tigers express the powerfulness "of an ego . . . licensed to thrust itself outward upon the world." Capable of projecting such an image, the poetic consciousness of Adrienne Rich moves toward its more open assertion. In future volumes, she will reject what the tigers represent as too controlling. At this stage, she knows only that sort of power, as "Mathilde in Normandy" demonstrates. Tellingly, this poem also depicts a creative woman. In "Mathilde in Normandy," as in "Aunt Jennifer's Tigers," the persona projects what she is denied onto her handiwork. Furthermore, this poem returns to the theme of "An Unsaid Word" by depicting the stay-at-home woman in contrast to the wandering man. In effect, "Mathilde in Normandy" synthesizes both previously mentioned poems and becomes more bold in its double-voiced discourse.

"Mathilde in Normandy" is based upon the popular legend that Queen Mathilde, the wife of William the Conqueror, created the Bayeaux Tapestry, which depicts the Norman Conquest of England. The poem is generated by the insight that great moments in history do not announce themselves as such to individuals living through them. The dominant voice asserts that women in particular may be faulted for not rising above "the personal episode" and for being blind to the great sweep of political events:

> Here is the threaded headland,
> The warp and woof of a tideless beach, the flight,
> Recounted by slow shuttles, of swift arrows,
> And the outlandish attitudes of death
> In the stitched soldiery. That this should prove
> More than the personal episode, more than all
> The little lives sketched on the teeming loom
> Was then withheld from you; self-conscious history
> That writes deliberate footnotes to its action
> Was not of your young epoch. For a pastime
> The patient handiwork of long-sleeved ladies
> Was esteemed proper when their lords abandoned

The fields and apple trees of Normandy
For harsher hunting on the opposite coast.

By the end of the poem, some revision in the original intent has
taken place. Signaled first by a shift in focus to "The patient
handiwork of long-sleeved ladies," a subject that seems a diver-
sion from the main intent, this revision gathers momentum
when the speaker interrupts the beautiful flow of imagery ("the
bright sun on the expensive threads / Glowed in the long wind-
less afternoons") and counters abruptly ("Say what you will,
anxiety there too / Played havoc with the skein"). Up to this
point, the person addressed in the poem has been Mathilde:
"was then withheld from *you*, " "Was not of *your* young epoch,"
and "*Yours* was a time when women sat at home." When the
speaker says, "Say what *you* will," the reader cannot be sure
who is being addressed. Mathilde is silent, her feelings "too
sharp for speech." No, the *you* being addressed here is the dominant voice in the poem.

The muted voice counters the dominant voice, emerging more
bravely as the speaker ventures compassion for Mathilde's anxiety and "the knots [which] came / When fingers' occupation
and mind's attention / Grew too divergent." Domestic life seems
calm and pleasant on the surface with its music, its "bright sun,"
and the women's weaving. But the speaker cannot ignore the
anxiety beneath this peaceful surface, especially when she conveys Mathilde's thought that her husband might never return
from the "void." The intimate understanding of the speaker's
tone, its patience with mistakes, its scrupulous attention to the
details of memory (the "wooden ships," "grey ocean dimming,"
and "sick strained farewells") is opposed to the distance of the
earlier section where the dominant voice articulates its theme in
abstract terms: "personal episode," "little lives," "self-conscious
history," "deliberate footnotes," and "young epoch." At the
same time, the speaker criticizes the "self-consciousness" of
modern times. The reader feels well-instructed, but little else.
Indeed, the sentiments come close to those Auden espouses in
his introduction to this volume. He praises Adrienne Rich's

craft: "In a young poet, as T. S. Eliot has observed, the most promising sign is craftsmanship for it is evidence of a capacity for detachment from the self and its emotions without which no art is possible."

Rich's incipient feminism, her advocacy of personal feeling in the creation of art, and her subtle advancement of women's handiwork as a valid art form pass undetected in this praise of her formal control. As readers we suspect that Rich's development as a feminist visionary did not begin sometime in the sixties. Signs of it can be found even in her early emulation of the formalism of those poets whom she admired. About this aspect of her career, she later says that "formalism was part of the strategy: like asbestos gloves it allowed me to handle materials I couldn't pick up bare-handed" (*ARP,* p. 94). Certainly the choice of a persona could be termed a strategic device. Not only is Mathilde someone other than the poet, she comes from a different epoch. Distance is thus doubly achieved. Rich can make a statement about women and creative power without being too "personal." Her command of blank verse that never descends to rhythmic monotony rings solidly through even the line which shifts the poem to its muted voice: "Say what you will, anxiety there too." Nothing in the poem calls attention to itself, except the beauty of the imagery and the strength of feeling at closure. It is the accomplishment expected from one who has earned the approval of W. H. Auden. If there are "knots" in this poem, they slip by without much notice. So, too, the muted voice, if we are not aware of the creative ingenuity demanded of the woman writer. If Adrienne Rich can say that "formalism was part of the strategy" that enabled her to handle certain unorthodox materials, the truth of her statement can be easily borne out.

Beside her ready accomplishment in poetic forms, nothing more was expected from Adrienne Rich, so nothing more was seen. She came at the end of a line of great modern poets, as Auden points out. She comes at the beginning of a great new age in poetry, one which will see women's poetry come to the forefront, one heralded by a double-voiced discourse so formally rendered it can hardly be detected. Mathilde's experience *is* "more than a personal episode" not simply because it fits into a larger historical moment, but because her experience encapsulates the common experience of women, including Adrienne Rich. First, Mathilde exists for love, depending for her happiness on a man—her lord. Second, she and the speaker regard the work Mathilde does with her hands not as art but as a "pastime," proper for ladies. Third, her work expresses her creative power and her envy of man's freedom to roam, to fight, to vanquish, but she cannot acknowledge this. Finally, her personal feelings intrude upon her work: knots come into the tapestry when Mathilde thinks too much about the poignant farewell scene, "too sharp for speech." About these common experiences, Mathilde is silent.

Adrienne Rich's poetry moves from this silence to an aesthetic that validates Mathilde's "pastime"—"the patient handiwork" involved in such women's art as weaving. Her poetry breaks away from the unquestioning admiration for the power that destroys toward a new definition of power based upon a woman's capacity to feel the particularity and commonality of female experience. Such feeling makes the character less skillful in this early poem—as if personal feeling cannot and should not be involved in the creation of valid art forms. Adrienne Rich takes the poem "Mathilde in Normandy" and turns it inside out. The poetic consciousness of the poet grows increasingly fascinated with the knots in such a tapestry as Mathilde weaves. Ultimately she transforms the image of female handiwork into an activity connected to the propagation of life itself, as in the following passage from the 1978 poem "Natural Resources":

> this weaving, ragged because incomplete
> we turn our hands to, interrupted
>
> over and over, handed down
> unfinished, found in the drawer
>
> of an old dresser in the barn,
> her vanished pride and care
>
> still urging us, urging on
> our works, to close the gap

in the Great Nebula,
to help the earth deliver.

While "this weaving" contains no observable knots, it is "ragged" and requires "our" (women's) attention to complete it. Rich attaches this "work" of the common woman to a cosmic vision involving the perpetuation of life itself. Woman becomes midwife in a metaphor of evolution tied to a new understanding of womanly power "to help the earth deliver." In the progression from "Mathilde in Normandy" to "Natural Resources," the poet's focus upon weaving as metaphor for ordinary female creativity ultimately brings Adrienne Rich to her mature awareness of the kind of power necessary for the survival and evolution of the world.

In conclusion, these three poems from *A Change of World* provide evidence of an early stage in Rich's evolution toward an aesthetics of power. Well-mannered and feminine on the surface, seemingly content with passivity, dependence, and restraint, these poems speak differently in their muted stories. Because two of them concern woman as artist, they communicate through their images the power that the woman artist feels, but dares not express overtly—at least in America in 1951. As aspects of the dominant story we find feminine docility, "fluttering" hands, and genteel manners. Alongside the dominant voice, these poems present a female imagination capable of hostility against repression, the strength of tigers, and the cruelty of an invading army. No wonder Rich's poems lie in feminine fashion about these hidden urges.

Since all these poems operate upon restraint (in style, in feeling, in objectivity) and strategies of disguise (for example, in choice of persona), they provide a clear picture of woman's negative experience of power. Further complicating the issue, Rich sees power as virility. In one sense, then, the ambivalence toward such power in her first book is true to Rich's ultimate vision that patriarchal, controlling power is fundamentally inimical to woman and to life on this planet. *A Change of World* thus exhibits early signs of the direction that Rich's poetry will take toward the definition and enactment of a beneficent female power.

An older Adrienne Rich, looking back upon the work of women writers like herself, explains how "the specter . . . of male judgment along with the active discouragement and thwarting of her needs by a culture controlled by males, has created problems for the woman writer: problems of contact with herself, problems of language and style, problems of energy and survival" (*ARP*, p. 92). Rich's understanding of these problems stems, of course, from her own grappling with them, a process that can be seen more vividly in her early poems than in her later feminist work when she throws off "the specter."

CHAPTER 3

THE CAREFUL
ARRIVISTE:
*THE
DIAMOND
CUTTERS*
(1955)

IN 1955, Adrienne Rich published a book of traditional, male-influenced poems in *The Diamond Cutters*. Rich's mimicry of her poetic mentors provides little indication of her later distinctiveness as a feminist poet, and understandably so. As a woman writing in a male-dominated culture and deeply influenced by the poetry of Frost, Stevens, Auden, Yeats, and Eliot, Rich quite naturally imitated their subject matter and style.[1] Even so, her mimicry gives way to subversion of her models and, to a certain extent, of patriarchal values. In examining the influences on Rich's poetry, the deviations from those influences assume particular importance, especially in the formulation of the feminist vision she inevitably moves toward, the core of which is womanly power.

Randall Jarrell reviewed *The Diamond Cutters* in 1956 for the *Yale Review,* and while he did not find a powerful, original poet, he did discover an "enchanting" one. He cites the perfections of Rich's craft and finds behind her poems' "clarity and gravity" a poet who seems a "princess in a fairy tale." She is a bit too perfect for Jarrell, and he wishes for a few interesting "imperfections." Later in his review he comes back to this theme, saying that "some part of me wants the poet less ideally normal than she is." Jarrell ends his review with a compliment for this good, young poet: "she deserves Shakespeare's favorite adjective, *sweet*" (*ARP*, p. 129). While the sexism and condescension of Jarrell's review seem blatant today, his remarks should not be dismissed outright. Feminist literary criticism allows a reader to see the poet Jarrell wished for but could not locate in *The Diamond Cutters*. Such criticism would take Rich's technical brilliance as a given, the natural consequence of the talented poet's knowledge of the modern poets she read and imitated. Other consequences of that imitation, however, would come under closer scrutiny.

Mimicry and its consequences for the woman writer are the subjects of Mary Jacobus's "The Question of Language," an article on George Eliot's *The Mill on the Floss*. Jacobus points out that "women have access to language only by recourse to systems of representation which are masculine" (*Writing and Sexual Difference*, p. 40). Jacobus does not subscribe to theories of a distinct woman's language; she assumes woman's mimicry of man's language. Within that mimicry, which Jacobus calls "an acting out or role playing within the text," the woman writer has certain leeway that marks her distinctiveness as a writer. Mimicry of male models, says Jacobus, "allows the woman writer the better to know and hence to expose what it is she mimics" (p. 40). Although Jacobus clarifies her thesis with reference to George Eliot and the novel, her theory of mimicry can be applied to the poetry of Adrienne Rich, particularly in early work as derivative as *The Diamond Cutters*.

Within Rich's mimicry of her male models lie deviations that Mary Jacobus would call "errors." Jacobus says that "Error . . . must creep in where there's a story to tell, especially a woman's story" (p. 48). Margaret Homans reinforces this point in her exploration of Wordsworth's influence on George Eliot, an influence to which Eliot had an ambivalent response. Homans explains that "though Eliot might like to write in congruence with a revered male authority, . . . she cannot and does not want to do so in . . . gendered matters" (p. 70). In *The Diamond Cutters*, poems that deal with "gendered matters" hold the key to those interesting "errors" that make Adrienne Rich less a fairy-tale princess and more a poet on her way toward discovering a female aesthetic.

Error, sin, and degeneration occupy the poetic consciousness of Rich as central metaphors in *The Diamond Cutters*. Take, for example, poems such as "Living in Sin" and "From the Land of Sinners." She addresses Satan himself in "Lucifer in the Train," finding him the prototype of all mortals, for "Once out of heaven, to an angel's eye / Where is the bush or cloud without a flaw?" The world of *The Diamond Cutters*, as Albert Gelpi states, is a "fallen world" (*ARP*, p. 132). In this world, not even love retains the purity of an ideal, for "to love a human face was to discover / The cracks of paint and varnish on the brow," as the speaker explains in "The Snow Queen." In such a fallen, flawed, cracked, error-ridden world, it behooves the artist to be "care-ful," as the title poem commands. Only in art, it seems, can there be perfection, happily a flawed aesthetic refuted by Rich's less-than-perfect mimicry of her male models. Not mistakes—certainly not a backsliding from moral rectitude or even those flaws that, we are told, make us human—Rich's errors are lapses from "congruence with a revered male authority" in poems that deal with matters of gender. Two poems clearly influenced by Robert Frost, "Autumn Equinox" and "The Perennial Answer," serve as illustrations of Rich's lapses. These poems treat a "woman's story," in both instances the story of a wife in a less-than-perfect marriage. To Randall Jarrell, "The Perennial Answer" is "typical neurotic-violent Frost." He describes "Autumn Equinox" as "almost the best Frost-influenced poem I've ever read" (*ARP*, p. 128).

"Autumn Equinox" is a good starting place, therefore, to explore the extent of Frost's influence on Rich and the "errors," if any, that creep into her mimicry. The prosodic influence is obvious, for this long narrative poem is appropriately rendered in Frostian blank verse. The long interior monologue is broken in one key place by dialogue. We hear echoes of "After Apple Picking" in the opening, which establishes a New England setting and a persona who works outside during the change of season:

The leaves that shifted overhead all summer
Are marked for earth now, and I bring the baskets
Still dark with clingings of another season
Up from the cellar.

The earth's season mimics the season of the old, retired couple in the poem, a Frostian commonplace. In contrast to "Apple Picking" or a poem such as "Mending Wall," the worker is a woman. Yet Frost has female persona poems too and "Autumn Equinox" echoes his compassion for the wife in "The Hill Wife," echoing as well the husband and wife dialogues that we find in Frost's "West-Running Brook" and "Home Burial."

In "Autumn Equinox," Adrienne Rich may find her structure and strategy in the example of Frost's poems, but she elects different points of emphasis. Her speaker, a woman beyond fifty, is married to a professor, as was Rich. Unlike Rich, the woman has no children, a fact about which she is curiously silent. This silence could be construed as the poet's attempt to make her poem different from Frost's "Home Burial," where the death and burial of a child is the locus of tension between husband and wife. In Frost's poem the wife's silence about her inner life drives the husband to beseech her to talk to him about the dead child. He says,

"My words are nearly always an offense.
I don't know how to speak of anything
So as to please you. But I might be taught
I should suppose. I can't say I see how.
A man must partly give up being a man
With women-folk."

The tensions between husband and wife in "Home Burial" finally erupt when she accuses him of callousness both in his digging of the child's grave and in the ordinary words he spoke afterward. At the end, the wife makes a move to leave her husband and he threatens, "I'll follow and bring you back by force. I will!—" The eruptions in this Frost poem contrast dramatically with the silences in Rich's.

The silence about children in Rich's "Autumn Equinox" could

mean anything or nothing. Once silence is recognized, however, it opens up the poem to further interpretation. Tillie Olsen's *Silences* explores "The power and need to create, over and beyond reproduction [which] is native in both women and men. Where the gifted among women (and men) have remained mute or have never attained full capacity, it is because of circumstances, inner or outer, which oppose the needs of creation."[2] Because of its silences about children and other "gendered matters," "Autumn Equinox" subverts the skillful Frost mimicry, raising questions about marriage, frustrated creativity, and the potential for change in men and women.

The first section of the poem describes the old couple's situation, the nature of their relationship, and their different personalities. The dominant motif is contrast: the woman is outside; Lyman, her husband, is in his study. He is quiet and the wife notes that "All the house is still, / now that I've left it." When it begins to get dark, the wife is the one to "come indoors to light the lamps." The husband is absorbed in Dryden's *Satires*, so absorbed he would sit in the dark. The woman wonders about this interest of her husband—"that least acidulous of men." This thought leads her to consider a possible reversal in their personalities. His obsession with satire reminds her of herself as she used to be:

> While I, who spent my youth and middle-age
> In stubborness and railing, pass the time
> Now, after fifty, raking in the sun
> The leaves that sprinkle slowly on the grass,
> And feel their gold like firelight at my back,
> In slow preoccupation with September.

Obviously, she has changed, as Lyman has. Her change appears to be for the better. She has the qualities of life, motion and light; he is imaged as static—"eyes alone moving / Like a mended piece of old clockwork." He has grown bitter perhaps; she appears in harmony with nature, the leaves she rakes— "their gold like firelight at my back." The beauty of Rich's metaphor depicts the aging of this woman as a transformation: the

34

dross of her life—the leaves she rakes—rendered golden and creating a nimbus around her. She has left her husband behind; he is less than the man he used to be, less the "scholar." Retired now, he once had a professorship and respectable work; the wife was his attendant. She had no career, no children. There was every reason for this woman to take her life and squeeze it dry, for the man to move beyond her, outdistancing her in his mental and spiritual growth. Instead, the opposite happens. The center section of the poem explores possible reasons:

> For Lyman
> The world was all the distance he pursued
> From home to lecture-room, and home again.
> ·
> I bit my fingers, changed the parlor curtains
> To ones the like of which were never seen
> Along our grave and academic street.

Thus the woman defies convention while the husband becomes convention itself. She walks outside in the moonlight, imagines that "the moon must shine on finer things / I had not seen," and comes to detest the pictures hanging in Lyman's study—"the crazy tower of Pisa," the "Pyramids," and "Cologne Cathedral."

> I hated them
> For priggishly enclosing in a room
> The marvels of the world, as if declaring
> Such was the right and fitting rôle of marvels.

If this could be called "typical neurotic Frost"—and I think Randall Jarrell's remark fits this poem as well as "The Perennial Answer"—it also allows Adrienne Rich "the better to know and hence to expose what it is she mimics." Perhaps "expose" is not the most appropriate word, as if Rich were revealing something that Frost deliberately kept hidden. As we have seen, he explores in "Home Burial" both sides of the husband/wife quarrel. Although he does get in his digs against women and marriage—"a man must partly give up being a man / With women-folk"— Frost's sympathies appear to go to both partners. He also treats

35

woman's silence. Rich's "lapse" from her mentor is to deepen the quality of silence.

In "Autumn Equinox" we have a woman who hates the confinement of "marvels," in effect the shrinkage of life. Her husband's taste for decoration leads to the confinement and is a reflection of his mind and habits—he who travels "all the distance" from his home to his classroom. The woman obviously feels ambivalent about her husband and her marriage, but never voices this to him. Nor does she go crazy, hence the profundity of the silence in a poem that condemns marriage as constricting while advancing an image of a woman as the embodiment of life itself and a symbol of transformation.

Adrienne Rich understands silences that proceed from woman's conditioning, particularly when such silences preserve a marriage. In general, Rich pays close attention to what goes "unsaid" by lies, secrets, and silences—the title of the 1979 collection of her selected prose. In most instances, women are the ones singled out for what they do not say, but not as objects of contempt. Such is the case in the key section of "Autumn Equinox" when the wife recalls a scene from her young married life after her experience of loathing for her husband's pictures:

> Night, and I wept aloud; half in my sleep,
> Half feeling Lyman's wonder as he leaned
> Above to shake me. "Are you ill, unhappy?
> Tell me what I can do."
> "I'm sick, I guess—
> I thought that life was different than it is."
> "Tell me what's wrong. Why can't you ever say?
> I'm here, you know."
> Half shamed, I turned to see
> The lines of grievous love upon his face,
> The love that gropes and cannot understand.
> "I must be crazy, Lyman—or a dream
> Has made me babble things I never thought.
> Go back to sleep—I won't be so again."

In this exchange, the significant turn comes when Lyman asks her to tell him "what's wrong." Evidently she is not crying for the first time and he accuses her, "Why can't you ever say? / I'm here, you know." Of course, that is the point. He is there, loving her, and she cannot say that his love does not satisfy her longing for uncontained "marvels." She must also regret her child-lessness, but about this the poem remains silent. To resent her marriage when her husband obviously loves her makes her think she "must be crazy." Is not his love enough? What else could she want? Vague and insubstantial, her needs do not have the weight of Lyman's love. So this woman smothers her discontent and opts for silence.

A brief comparison with the dialogue between a husband and wife in "West-Running Brook" will highlight Rich's handling of the woman's silence and clarify her deviation from the Frost in-fluence. In the middle of the Frost poem, the wife claims that she had a vision of the brook "in an annuciation." The husband resents her claim as being too exclusively female.

> "Oh, if you take it off to lady-land,
> As't were the country of the Amazons
> We men must see you to the confines of
> And leave you there, ourselves forbid to enter,—
> It is your brook! I have no more to say."

Although the husband negates the woman's vision in a sexual put-down, the woman does not seem to notice. All she seems to hear is his offended male pride and she moves to boost him up. When he exclaims that he has "no more to say," she encourages him: "Yes, you have, too. Go on. You thought of something." And, of course, he has. Her prompting encourages him to deliver a long and beautiful interpretation of the wave and rock as meta-phor. Though the poem resolves itself in what they both said about the brook, the husband gets the best lines. He has some-thing to say and no trouble saying it. Plus he has the support and encouragement of the woman—that is, this poem says nothing remarkable about traditional sex roles.

In Rich's poem, the dialogue appears more honest, the people less stick figures set up by the poet to present a predetermined discourse. If the wife in "West-Running Brook" seems a male fantasy of female acquiescence to male superiority, the wife in Rich's poem appears more complex in her acquiescence, more human in her recognition of the difficult choices a woman must make in a marriage that threatens to confine her and to shrink possibility. When the wife in "Autumn Equinox" recognizes "The lines of grievous love" on her husband's face, his sensitivity and caring, even though his love "gropes and can not understand," she gives in to him and to their marriage. Telling him to "Go back to sleep," she silences her discontent.

If anything, the comparison with the Frost dialogue is unfair to Frost. His probing of neurotic relationships led Rich to do the same, but not as a side issue as in "West-Running Brook." It is not just that Rich gives a woman's perspective, bringing to it the authority of her own experience. In this particular comparison, her insight into womanly silence is more keen, less fraught with stereotypical views. Further on, the speaker in "Autumn Equinox" asks young lovers who marry to consider "that each must know / Beyond a doubt what's given, what received?" It is clear that the wife in her poem gave herself up to her husband's love. She also gave up her longing for a larger life in the world. This exchange culminates in stoic resignation for both of them, as the last section of the poem makes clear:

> Now we are old like Nature; patient, staid,
> Unhurried from the year's wellworn routine,
> We wake and take the day for what it is,
> And sleep as calmly as the dead who know
> They'll wake to their reward.

The comparison of their lives to Nature and the peculiar New England brand of their stoic resignation are Frostian, typical, and not very interesting. The silences in the poem are more telling. They give us a clue to Rich's lapses from Frost's influence and mark the poem as characteristic of her development not just as a writer who must subvert her influences in order to establish her own poetic identity, but also as a feminist visionary who knows woman's silences from within and whose quest is to transform those silences.

"The Perennial Answer" provides further evidence of Frost's influence on Rich and how she subverts that influence with her own emphasis on woman's silence, unbroken or broken. In the voice of an aging widow, this interior monologue tells the story of a marriage in a rural New England setting. Thus Rich takes geography from Frost along with the iambic pentameter, the rhymes, and the soliloquies. The tone is as blunt and austere as the people's lives. The poem opens, for example, with the woman defining herself as one who would "have the blackest word told straight, / Whether it was my child that couldn't live / Or Joel's mind, thick-riddled like a sieve / With all that loving festered into hate." Within the atmosphere of "neurotic-violent Frost," two significant themes emerge: the emphasis on the "blackest *word* told straight" and the stark mentioning (never brought up again) of the dead child. If the previous poem was silent about child-lessness, this poem is terse. In both poems childlessness remains a background issue, its meaning elusive. A child is a concrete, living manifestation of woman's creative power. For centuries, of course, children were regarded as the primary vehicle of womanly power. The implication in both poems is that a woman's power lies not simply in children, which she may or may not have, but in her words, unspoken or spoken. "The Perennial Answer" gives us both.

The unspoken word comes up first. The married couple lives in an atmosphere of rigid restraint in which horror and violence emerge as central events. Joel the husband is the only one of the farmers not afraid of "the idiot killer" hiding in the barn. When he emerges from having "brought the fellow out," he turns to his wife for her acknowledgment. She will not give it to him:

> . . . as if by rights his wife
> Should go to him for having risked his life
> And say—I hardly knew what thing he wanted.
> I know it was a thing I never granted.

The wife's withholding of her speech—her unsaid word—be-comes the source of her power. Cruel as this is, neurotic and perverted to boot, it is her only way to maintain her sense of herself in a marriage that feels like "a room so strange and lonely / She looked outside for warmth." The man she finds is a preacher and the poem's trope for him is similar to the room image above. He is a "man of God indeed, / . . . whose heart / Thrust all it knew of passion into one / Chamber of iron inscribed *Thy will be done*." We are in Hawthorne-land, but worse.

When the woman walks home late one night with her preacher, Joel rapes her: "I knew / that he could kill me then, but what he did / Was wrench me up the stairs, onto the bed." The woman does not run away as does Frost's "Hill Wife" in a rough parallel; instead she endures. Joel dies before she does. The emotional center of this poem occurs toward the end when the woman recounts the night of her husband's death:

> I slept alone
> In this same room. A neighbor said she'd stay,
> Thinking the dead man lying down below
> Might keep the living from rest. She told me so:
> "Those hours before the dawn can lie like stone
> Upon the heart—I've lain awake—I know."
> At last I had to take the only way,
> And said, "The nights he was alive and walking
> From room to room and hearing spirits talking,
> What sleep I had was likelier to be broken."
> Her face was shocked but I was glad I'd spoken.
> "Well, if you feel so—" She would tell the tale
> Next morning, but at last I was alone
> In an existence finally my own.

In this section, Rich returns to the image of "An Unsaid Word" with several crucial differences. The man wanders in an intensity close to madness: "hearing spirits talking." The woman does not "stand where he left her, still his own," but breaks away into "an existence finally my own." Her entry into this existence is brought on by what she says: it is "the only way." Her speaking out risks the convention of wifely loyalty and she recognizes that her neighbor "was shocked."

Rich's poem does not imagine that the woman estranged from

her husband might find more than funereal sympathy in her neighbor. As yet, Adrienne Rich has no inkling of a dream of a common language that might unite women and bring into existence "the unsaid word." The "existence finally my own" is separate not just from an oppressive, brutal husband but from other women. Thus Rich's speaker lacks awareness of the commonality of woman's negative experience of power. Similarly lacking is a drive to connect Rich's sense of herself as a woman with her role as a poet. That is, she does not bring this desire to conscious expression. Instead, her persona speaks words ("The nights he was alive . . .") that abjure the lies and secrets which held her marriage together. With the absence of the man, she can speak. Obviously woman, like man, requires solitude ("at last I was alone") in order to engage in the quest for the self ("in an existence finally my own"). The words that break the silence of complicity initiate the action. Thus Rich's persona takes the steps that the poet will ultimately take in her development as a woman poet. That is, she will come to base her aesthetic upon her sense of being a woman with a woman's own power—not something siphoned off from a man. As yet, she still regards maleness as power.

In her essay "The Kingdom of the Fathers," Rich suggests that "the idea of power has, for most women, been inextricably linked with maleness, or the use of force; most often, with both" (p. 24). In "The Snow Queen," also from *The Diamond Cutters,* she gives us a poetic realization of this key insight. The poem's first three lines locate us firmly in the Hans Christian Andersen tale from which it gets its title: "Child with a chip of mirror in his eye / Saw the world ugly, fled to plains of ice / Where beauty was the Snow Queen's promises." Then it takes as its central trope the "chip of mirror" that gave the child a distorted impression of the world; for the speaker, this is "a splinter sharp as his. . . ." The remainder of the poem is filled with perverse images, clear and grave:

> In the deceptive province of my birth
> I had seen yes turn no, the saints descend,
> Their sacred faces twisted into smiles,

> The stars gone lechering, the village spring
> Gush mud and toads—all miracles
> Befitting an incalculable age.

As part of the "fallen world" of *The Diamond Cutters,* this poem has a definable place. Yet our experience of the whole poem leads us to reject a superficial interpretation, in part because certain elements of it appear inscrutable. The speaker addresses an unknown "you" in the poem. Although we can probably assume that the speaker is female, only toward the end does her female identity become discernible. Her relationship with the "you" defines her key dilemma. As long as she maintains this relationship, she has not completely surrendered herself to a perverse vision of the world: "In you belonged simplicities of light / To mend distraction, teach the air / To shine, the stars to find their way again." Thus the "you" takes on benevolent qualities ascribed by the speaker: it can "mend" and "teach." If the speaker gives up the "you," she will have renounced these qualities.

At this juncture in the poem, the Snow Queen asserts herself, her power clearly superior to the speaker's other allegiance:

> Yet here the Snow Queen's cold prodigious will
> Commands me, and your face has lost its power,
> Dissolving to its opposite like the rest.
> Under my ribs a diamond splinter now
> Sticks, and has taken root; I know
> Only this frozen spear that drives me through.

In this climactic section, the speaker's emphasis falls upon the "diamond splinter," and we imagine her as being impaled on the "frozen spear," a phallic image. The "you" dissolves as the splinter "sticks." The speaker is touched to the core—not simply in the eye, as was the boy. Even so, her wound energizes her; she says it "drives me through." It is also beautiful and precious, the qualities we ascribe to diamonds. A beautiful wounding that does not make the speaker a victim makes sense only if we identify the speaker as female.

The real subject of Adrienne Rich's poem is female creativity.

The speaker's wound is her acknowledgment of the creative power that has energized her. That power is male and forceful. As Susan Gubar writes in "The Blank Page and The Issues of Female Creativity," "one of the primary and most resonant metaphors provided by the female body is blood, and cultural forms of creativity are often experienced as a painful wounding" (*Writing and Sexual Difference*, p. 78). Though we do not find any blood in "The Snow Queen," we are made graphically aware of the wound sustained by the speaker. Rich's poem provides a clear demonstration of Gubar's insight. Otherwise, it remains inscrutable.

If this interpretation seems too far-fetched, we might see how it helps us to perceive the poem's relationship to the others previously discussed. In those poems, female expression was stunted; in this one, the speaker experiences a searing wound. In all three poems, the woman endures, sometimes stunningly. The triumph is even more striking in "The Snow Queen" because the male influence has "taken root" and has been transmogrified. Echoes of other poets are minuscule or absent. As Susan Gubar explains about the woman artist, "artistic creation often feels like a violation, a belated reaction to male penetration rather than a possessing and controlling. . . . Women's paint and ink are produced through a physical wounding, a literal influence of male authority" (*Writing and Sexual Difference*, p. 86). In the two Frost-influenced poems there were few, if any, forms of self-expression available to the woman. Silence, therefore, became a potent metaphor. The influence of Frost and other poets on Adrienne Rich, however, leads to the release of her creative power, as the "The Snow Queen" attests.

The title poem of *The Diamond Cutters* advances our understanding of that power through its central metaphor. This poem appears to emerge from a perception about the craft required for an artisan to work with the material at hand and transform it into something that can be called a work of art. It is no quirk that Rich chooses diamond cutting as her central metaphor. This poem can be regarded as a companion piece to "The Snow Queen," for it picks up on the diamond nature of the "splinter" that pierces Rich's persona as well as the coldness of the diamond. Though "the stone is just a stone," it has not crumbled as have "The mountain and the pebble— / But not this coldest one."

The formality of "The Diamond Cutters" takes a different shape from the Frost-influenced poems or even "The Snow Queen," its closest relative in this volume. Rich employs iambic trimeters throughout and the shortness of the line creates a clipped, almost abrupt rhythm from which we gain our impression of the speaker—a no-nonsense, but kindly authoritarian. Apparently an experienced diamond cutter, the speaker addresses a silent "you," named at one point a "careful arriviste." To the neophyte, the speaker gives a series of directions. For example, the newcomer must "Be serious," "Be hard of heart," "Keep your desire apart," "Love only what you do, / And not what you have done," "Be proud." The listener could well be a young poet receiving instruction in the poetic craft.

The voice in the poem encompasses a vast expanse of time. Stanza 2 conveys the sweep of its knowledge:

> Now, you intelligence
> So late dredged up from dark
> Upon whose smoky walls
> Bison took fumbling form
> Or flint was edged on flint—
> Now, careful arriviste,
> Delineate at will
> Incisions in the ice.

If we accept diamond cutting as a metaphor for the creative process, the godlike voice appears to be the spirit of poetry, in effect a poetic muse. Traditionally, the muse is a female deity; here, the muse is a paterfamilias, authoritative and demanding. It sets high standards: "Respect the adversary, / Meet it with tools refined, / And thereby set your price." It is emotionally restrained: "Keep your desire apart. / Love only what you do, / And not what you have done." In sum, the muse embodies a traditional form of masculine power.

44

In adopting this masculine voice, Rich asserts an inextricable connection between masculinity and the creative process. With the masculine power of intelligence, will, and control the "careful arriviste" can make "incisions in the ice," a trope for the creation of a work of art. Rich's thinking along these lines parallels the passage quoted from *The Second Sex* in which Simone de Beauvoir traces the development of man's creativity to his mastery of tools in the Bronze Age. De Beauvoir's analysis, contrary to Rich's at this point, dwells upon such mastery as the turning point in woman's relegation to a lesser status of being. Without a similar feminist consciousness, Adrienne Rich in "The Diamond Cutters" assumes the superiority of "the male principle of creative force, of light, of intelligence, of order."

It is difficult to imagine the woman in "Autumn Equinox" performing the acts that Rich's speaker requires in "The Diamond Cutters." Her control turns inward upon the self in various forms of restraint and disguise. In contrast, Rich's poetic muse demands the kind of control that turns outward and liberates "pure and expensive fires / Fit to enamor Shebas." This gesture captures what Rich has said about woman's sense of man's powerfulness: "the expressive energy of an ego which, unlike ours, was licensed to thrust itself outward upon the world" ("The Kingdom of the Fathers," p. 23).

It is not difficult to imagine the formal stylist of all the poems in this volume subscribing to the aesthetic of "The Diamond Cutters." The poetic theory articulated here is traditional and familiar to readers of modern poetry. Rich herself admits in "When We Dead Awaken" (1971) that her "style was formed first by male poets: . . . Frost, Dylan Thomas, Donne, Auden, MacNiece, Stevens, Yeats." She also says that what she "chiefly learned from them was craft" (*ARP*, p. 94). As for women poets, she looked "for the same things [she] had found in the poetry of men, because [she] wanted women poets to be the equals of men, and to be equal was still confused with sounding the same" (p. 94).

What a woman poet would sound like when she was not trying to sound the same as a man is, of course, something that Adrienne Rich could not begin to articulate in 1955, the time of *The Diamond Cutters*. Although Rich's lapses from Frost, as I have shown, connect a woman's silence with her power and, in the case of "The Perennial Answer," connect a woman's breaking of that silence with her coming into "an existence finally my own," the two poems in this volume which deal with the poet's own creative power do not connect that power with anything womanly. Granted, the Snow Queen is a female power, but she utilizes it as force. As yet, therefore, Rich does not connect a woman's sounds with the sources of her power as a poet.

The lies, secrets, and silences of the women in her poems create a strangulation miles away from the music of poetry. Looking back upon the period of *The Diamond Cutters*, Adrienne Rich writes:

> I have a sense that women didn't talk to each other much in the fifties—not about their secret emptinesses, their frustrations. I went on trying to write; my second book and first child appeared in the same month. But by the time that book came out I was already dissatisfied with those poems, which seemed to me mere exercises for poems I hadn't written. The book was praised, however, for its "gracefulness"; I had a marriage and a child. If there were doubts, if there were periods of null depression or active despairing, these could only mean that I was ungrateful, insatiable, perhaps a monster. (*ARP*, p. 95)

Rich suggests that, for her, not talking to other women about "secret emptinesses" and "frustrations" led to poems which were "mere exercises." The beauty of many passages in these poems plus Rich's lapses from her poetic influences and the underlying integrity of her handling of "gendered matters" belie her negative self-estimation. These poems are more than exercises. Still, it follows that an environment of shared language with other women would be the most conducive to her growth as a poet and a woman.

As we have seen, Rich's instinctive originality in these early poems lies not in formal, stylistic matters, but in her special insight into what it means to be a woman in the kingdom of the fathers. Here, Adrienne Rich finds her subject. When she connects these insights with her considerable skill in the poetic craft, she begins to find her own voice.

CHAPTER 4

THE SONG
OF SILK:
*SNAPSHOTS
OF A
DAUGHTER-
IN-LAW*
(1963)

WHILE ADRIENNE RICH produced her first two books of poems in four years, her third book, *Snapshots of a Daughter-in-Law,* was delayed both for family reasons—she gave birth to three sons between 1955 and 1959—and for artistic reasons. She was freeing herself from her early poetic influences and shaping a new artistic self. As Albert Gelpi says, this is a "transitional" volume (*ARP,* p. 133), and in it we find metered poems with rhyme schemes as well as poems that do not scan easily because Rich is experimenting with a looser line. She also experiments with new subject matter. Many of these poems are not completely successful and the reader might come away from a first reading of this book wishing that Rich had stayed with what she did so well in *A Change of World* and *The Diamond Cutters.*

Aside from writing some awkward or incomplete poems in *Snapshots,* Rich takes on a male persona in many of her poems or otherwise sees herself as a man. Albert Gelpi justifies this male identification by applying a Jungian interpretation, saying that "the poet is at this point imagining herself in terms of her 'animus,' the archetypally 'masculine' component in the woman's psyche" (*ARP,* p. 137). In summing up the climate of the poems, Gelpi says: "The psychological and artistic point which the *Snapshots* volume dramatizes is Adrienne Rich's rejection of the terms on which society says we must expend our existence and her departure on an inner journey of exploration and discovery. As a woman-poet, she finds herself, perhaps unconsciously to a large extent, making the initial discoveries in the dimension and through the lead of her animus" (P. 138).

A closer look at key poems in *Snapshots* will show that the male persona poems as well as the title poem which treats women's selves as costumes are not simply "animus" poems, but that Rich is developing a radical sense of the nature of the self which points beyond the "androgynous wholeness" of Jungian psychology toward a feminist vision where the self is not locked into gender-specific roles. In her treatment of identity and of costumes of the self, Adrienne Rich participates in a vision of the world and the self found in feminist modernists like Virginia Woolf.

In the essay "Costumes of the Mind: Transvestism as Metaphor in Modern Literature," Sandra M. Gilbert presents the theory that male modernists like Joyce, Lawrence, and T. S. Eliot treat literal and figurative costumes in a different manner from feminist modernists like Woolf, H.D., and Djuna Barnes. Gilbert's thesis can also be borne out by key poems from Adrienne Rich's *Snapshots,* in which she often assumes a male persona, sees herself as a man, or treats women's selves as costumes, thus fluid and changeable. In Gilbert's essay she quotes the famous lines from Yeats's "Sailing to Byzantium":

> An aged man is but a paltry thing,
> A tattered coat upon a stick, unless
> Soul clap its hands and sing, and louder sing,
> For every tatter in its mortal dress.

This metaphor, Gilbert says, "posits a heart's truth which stands apart from false costumes" (*Writing and Sexual Difference,* p. 193). In a feminist work such as Woolf's *Orlando,* however, we find a different perception of the relation of clothes to self. Woolf's hero becomes a heroine with the accompanying changes in costume, and the novel readily supports its narrator's view that "it is clothes that wear us and not we them. . . . We may make them take the mould of arm or breast, but [clothes] mould our hearts, our brains, our tongues to their liking."[1] If Yeats would lead us to believe that costumes may be false or true and that costumes are separate from the self, a feminist modernist like Woolf suggests that "we are what we wear" (*Writing and Sexual Difference*, p. 193).

Lest Gilbert be accused of taking Woolf's good-hearted romp, *Orlando*, too seriously, I quote in full what she says about costumes and the male modernists against which she juxtaposes the modernist and post-modernist women writers among whom Adrienne Rich must be included:

> Literary men, working variations upon the traditional dichotomy of appearance and reality, often oppose false costumes to true clothing. Sometimes, they oppose costume (seen as false or artificial) to nakedness (which is true, "natural," and the equivalent of a suitable garment or guise). Frequently, moveover, they see false costumes as unsexed or wrongly sexed, transvestite travesties, while true costumes are properly sexed. In defining such polarities, all are elaborating a deeply conservative vision of society both as it is and as it should be, working, that is, on the assumption that the sociopolitical world should be hierarchical, orderly, stylized. Often, indeed, in their anxiety about the vertiginous freedom offered by an age of changing clothes, these men seem nostalgic for the old days of uniforms, and so they use costume in poems and novels in part to abuse them. Even more important, their obsessive use of sex-connected costumes suggests that for most male modernists the hierarchical order of society is and should be a pattern based upon gender distinctions, since the ultimate reality is in their view the truth of gender, a truth embodied or clothed in cultural paradigms which all these writers see as both absolute and Platonically ideal and which the most prominent among them—Joyce, Lawrence, Yeats, Eliot—continually seek to revive. (*Writing and Sexual Difference*, p. 195)

Stressing the "deeply conservative vision of society" presented by these literary men, one which locates its "ultimate reality" in "the truth of gender" (men are men and women are women and each sex has appropriate or "true" costumes), Gilbert challenges us to see their treatment of gender reality in a strikingly original way.

She contrasts these male modernists with their female counterparts who handle costume metaphor differently. "[They] not only regard all clothing as costume," writes Gilbert, but "they also define all costume as false." She continues:

> Yet [feminist modernists] don't oppose false costume to "true" nakedness, for to most of these writers that fundamental sexual self for which, say, Yeats uses nakedness as a metaphor is itself another costume. . . . Many literary women from Woolf to Plath see what literary men call "selves" as costumes and costumes as "selves," in a witty revision of male costume metaphors. . . . Moreover, . . . feminist modernist costume imagery is radically revisionary in a political as well as a literary sense, for it implies that no one, male or female, can or should be confined to a uni-form, a single form or self. On the contrary, . . . many twentieth-century women have struggled—sometimes exuberantly, sometimes anxiously—to define a gender-free reality behind or beneath myth, an ontological essence so pure, so free that "it" can "inhabit" any self, any costume. (p. 196)

These quotations from Gilbert's essay are long because of the complex, radical nature of her thesis, the crux of which is that literary women, contrary to their male counterparts, perceive the interchangeability of self and costume. For them, nakedness is no more "true" than its costume, nor should anyone "be confined to a uni-form, a single form or self." Thus these women challenge the males' perception of the ultimate reality of gender. Gender itself becomes a costume and everything is in a state of flux. If gender is not fixed, then costume does not become terribly significant; it can be treated, as Gilbert says, with "irony and ambiguity" (p. 195). This contrasts with the seriousness that male modernists attach to "properly sexed" costumes.

While Gilbert does not cite Adrienne Rich in her article, key poems in *Snapshots* bear out Gilbert's thesis and indicate that Rich must be included among those literary women who challenge the "fixity" of gender. Among the volume's earlier, more traditional poems, "The Knight" and "The Loser" stand out as male persona poems. In "The Loser," the title is followed by an explanatory note: "A man thinks of the woman he once loved: first, after her wedding, and then nearly a decade later." It appears to be influenced by the many Yeats poems about his hopeless love for Maud Gonne, particularly "The Folly of Being Comforted." In the second section of Rich's poem, the man says, "My envy is of no avail. / I turn my head and wish him well / who chafed your beauty into use." Along with the regular scansion, we note the end rhyme, relics not just of Yeatsian practice, but of Rich's style in her first two volumes.

"The Knight" (1957) is formal in the same fashion, but any direct influence is difficult to detect. It is a curious poem for Rich because its subject matter appears antique and outside of her usual interests. The impulse of the poem seems literary. As in a Medieval or Renaissance romance, the poem describes a knight in full armor going on a quest or to the joust. He presents a magnificent appearance, but we are shown less glamorous stuff underneath. The poem presents a contrast in its first two parts. The resplendent imagery of the opening stanza conveys a strong visual picture of the knight's armor. Not only does his helmet "point to the sun," but his mail seems to magnify the sun. Thus the poet creates an image of the solar figure of Jungian heroic myth. In images where "The soles of his feet glitter" and "his palms flash," she advances the sense of glory of the knightly progress. Even so, that glitter and flash are aspects of his armor, his costume, and not of him. In this manner, his costume dominates and creates his identity as a knight. To paraphrase Virginia Woolf, "his clothes wear him."

The second stanza provides ironic contrast to the first as the speaker gives us a closer, inside view of the knight. We get a look at his eye, "a lump of bitter jelly / set in a metal mask," and his underwear, a disgraceful set of "rags and tatters." Far from the chivalric picture painted in the first stanza, the knight's "nerves [are worn] to ribbons / under the radiant casque." As we hold both views of the knight in our minds—the external appearance and the inner reality—we might think that Rich is giving us a conventional rendering of the self versus the mask conflict. Thus the armor or costume is perceived as false while the nervous man beneath the armor constitutes the true self.

The poem may be read in this conventional manner, but it also conveys a female concern and a feminist insight. The questions of stanza 3 betray a female concern:

> Who will unhorse this rider
> and free him from between
> the walls of iron, the emblems
> crushing his chest with their weight?
> Will they defeat him gently,
> or leave him hurled on the green,
> his rags and wounds still hidden
> under the great breastplate?

In Carol Gilligan's *In a Different Voice,* she shows how the moral values and development of women differ from those of men, and characterizes women's values as "sensitivity to the needs of others and the assumption of responsibility for taking care."[2] Rich's speaker typifies these values. The speaker does not ask how the knight will overcome his nervousness and live up to the ideal of knighthood. In fact, the knight's defeat could lead to his freedom from his costume—his uni-form, those "walls of iron, the emblems / crushing his chest with their weight." The worst thing that could happen, and the speaker's grave, sad tone conveys this, would be for him to die in his armor, "his rags and wounds still hidden / under the great breastplate."

Rich's attitude toward manhood or manliness as power has taken a profound turn as she studies a quintessential manly role and sees it as nothing but a costume that should be thrown away. There is no nostalgia here for a world of lost values. Neither does the emphasis of the poem fall upon the difference between a false costume and a true one, but on freeing the self from the costume. In these respects, therefore, "The Knight" cuts deeply into a particular myth of manliness to suggest a reality beyond "proper" gender roles.

In "Antinoüs: The Diaries," a less formal, more passionate poem than "The Knight," Rich goes back even further into history to write a poem in the voice of "A beautiful youth, favorite boy of the Emperor Hadrian, who drowned in the Nile, perhaps a suicide, in A.D. 130." Rich glosses this footnote to the poem with, "I let the young man speak for me" (*ARP*, p. 16). Antinoüs is a male homosexual and since Rich has been open about her own lesbianism since the early seventies, we can only imagine that letting Antinoüs speak for her in 1959 was enormously liberating for her imagination. For this reason, among others, it is difficult to see this poem as simply an animus poem. Transitional in style as well as in content, it broaches the taboo subject of homosexuality.

In this poem, Rich imagines the kinds of thoughts that might have gone through the head of Antinoüs before he drowned, possibly a suicide. She probes the reasons why this beautiful, favored youth considered his life no longer worth living. Albert Gelpi points out that this poem "expresses . . . a revulsion against the middle-class, suburban life which traps women, either willingly or helplessly, in gestures and postures. In 'Antinoüs,' Rich speaks through the mask of a man, but as the favorite of the Emperor Hadrian, memorialized in busts for his sensual beauty, Antinoüs becomes the perverted image of the object of man's lust and so a mirror of a decadent society" (*ARP*, p. 136).

Except by implication, we do not learn much about homosexuality in this poem. Because Antinoüs is an outsider, however favored by the emperor, we do learn much about the society that encompasses him but has no idea what he thinks or feels. We are privileged for we can read his "Diaries"—those thoughts that he could only make known privately. Because of his "sensual beauty," no one cared if he had thoughts, secret or otherwise. Because of his position in society, opportunities for self-expression were minimal. Thus this homosexual outsider becomes an appropriate mask for a woman trapped in a sexist society.

The poem begins with an utterly bleak vision of the autumn season, lightened only by the speaker's joy in getting away by himself on an evening walk:

> Autumn torture. The old signs
> smeared on the pavement, sopping leaves
> rubbed into the landscape as unguent on a bruise,
> brought indoors, even, as they bring flowers, enormous,
> with the colors of the body's secret parts.
> All this. And then, evenings, needing to be out,
> walking fast, fighting the fire
> that must die, light that sets my teeth on edge with joy,
> till on the black embankment
> I'm a cart stopped in the ruts of time.

Rich begins with Antinoüs's reaction to autumn, his revulsion toward the "sopping leaves." These are "old signs" of decay, part of the process of nature that decrees a cycle in order for regeneration to take place. It is bad enough to see the "smeared" leaves outside on the city streets, but it appalls him further that they are sometimes brought inside as decoration, "as they bring flowers, enormous, / with the colors of the body's secret parts." This revulsion of Antinoüs's seems a little precious, what one might associate with a squeamish effete. It is more than that, however, for he associates these autumn colors with "the body's secret parts." The leaves must remind him of his function, which is to satisfy the lust of the emperor. Antinoüs has his own drives toward which he is ambivalent, "fighting the fire / that must die / light that sets my teeth on edge with joy." Because of his dependent status, of course, he cannot satisfy these drives. The first stanza culminates in the bleak metaphor: "I'm a cart stopped in the ruts of time." Antinoüs ends his night walks "on the black embankment" (of the Nile) contemplating, we must imagine, suicide. At least then he would have control over his own destiny.

Rich takes up this man's thoughts and tries them on as if they were "costumes of the mind." This chronicler of an effete revulsion is also the mother of three sons, the last born in 1959, the year of this poem. *Effete* derives from the Latin *effetus,* worn out by childbearing. In letting Antinoüs speak for her, Adrienne Rich expresses more than latent homosexuality. If Rich rejects "the terms on which society says we must expend our existence," those terms probably include the culmination of a woman's self in the roles of wife and mother. The images in the first stanza contain a revulsion against sex and the cycle of regeneration, for what are "the body's secret parts" but the genital organs? Set against these images are references to "fire" and the "light that sets my teeth on edge with joy." We could say that these terms refer to an illicit passion of some sort, but such passions must be the norm for Antinoüs. Thus the imagery must refer to a different sort of light. We get no further definition of this contrary element until stanza 2, when Antinoüs brings up the subject of poetry:

> Then at some house the rumor of truth and beauty
> saturates a room like lilac-water
> in the steam of a bath, fires snap, heads are high,
> gold hair at napes of necks, gold in glasses,
> gold in the throat, poetry of furs and manners.
> Why do I shiver then? Haven't I seen,
> over and over, before the end of an evening,
> the three opened coffins carried in and left in a corner?

Antinoüs, drawn inside by "the rumor of truth and beauty," finds nothing but a sham, a "poetry of furs and manners." Though "fires snap" at this poetry, Antinoüs is left cold. "Why do I shiver then?" he asks. Rich's wit provides us with a dazzling display of her language. She carries through the opening image of the "rumor of truth and beauty" that "saturates a room like lilac-water / in the steam of a bath," giving us not only the social atmosphere during the decadent period of the Roman Empire, but also delaying her point as she builds image upon golden image into a rococo of vulgar splendor. This "poetry of furs and manners" is some stylish thing, a glamorous costume that does nothing for Antinoüs but remind him again of death and decay. As "costume" it can be treated ironically. Besides, Antinoüs has other things on his mind that he cannot block out: "the three opened coffins carried in and left in a corner."

Antinoüs questions his own reactions, actually his lack of immunity to the death boxes introduced into the social chamber. Unlike the man who "cracked his shin / on one of them, winced and hopped and limped / laughing to lay his hand on a beautiful arm," Antinoüs "shivers" at the thought of death. Perhaps it is because he is still young. Certainly he has not been completely corrupted or he would not feel what he feels. Maybe, since it is suggested by Rich's choice of persona, he sees what he sees by reason of his "outsider" status, his homosexuality. Yet we do not discover a man who loves other men in this poem, but rather a thoughtful, sensitive boy who is loved by a special man. The poem skirts the subject of homosexuality to dwell upon being a "loved one" and the consequences of that kind of passive role, which is, in many respects, the woman's role.

The third stanza turns the poem in a new direction as Antinoüs challenges the truth of his own account:

> The old, needless story. For if I'm here
> it is by choice and when at last
> I smell my own rising nausea, feel the air
> tighten around my stomach like a surgical bandage,
> I can't pretend surprise. What is it I so miscarry?
> If what I spew on the tiles at last,
> helpless, disgraced, alone,
> is in part what I've swallowed from glasses, eyes,
> motions of hands, opening and closing mouths,
> isn't it also dead gobbets of myself,
> abortive, murdered, or never willed?

This writer of diaries could compose a different story, at least an ending of his own. The language of this section grows passionate as Antinoüs admits responsibility for decisions that have led him to his present condition. He does not wallow in his revulsion, nor does his disgust appear "effete" anymore. Rich's approach is visceral not precious. The images of vomiting join with other images of miscarriage—the birth that never comes to term, the conceived self that does not evolve into an existent being.

The impact of the poem is such that we forget about the real life resolution into suicide. Antinoüs, the male mask Rich chose for herself, develops the amazing strength to see his own participation in a life that is using him, putting him on, making him conform to its shape. The thrust of the poem is that he can throw this life off and thereby throw off the self he detests. A costume that does not fit can be changed. Thus the self of Antinoüs is not a fixed entity. The role he plays with its requisite costumes must and will be discarded. Rich uses vomiting as an extended metaphor to suggest that once this action begins there will be no rest until completion. In addition, the use of "miscarry" brings the poem into the realm of specifically female concerns.

The title poem, "Snapshots of a Daughter-in-Law," brings those female concerns to the fore. In its ten parts, Rich displays the same merciless examination and ironic wit, this time applied to the unrealized potential of women's lives.[3] A strong poem, "Snapshots" communicates an incensed frustration at woman's oppression and her complicity in it. As Antinoüs says, "For if I'm here, it is by choice." A visionary poem, "Snapshots" foresees woman's liberation into a pure being capable of taking on several different forms, as in the tenth and final section:

> Her mind full to the wind, I see her plunge
> breasted and glancing through the currents,
> taking the light upon her
> at least as beautiful as any boy
> or helicopter,
>   poised, still coming,
> her fine blades making the air wince
> but her cargo
> no promise then:
> delivered
> palpable
> ours.

In Rich's new, variable meter, her passionate speech rhythms, her striking images, she articulates an explicitly feminist vision that emphasizes woman's ability to transform herself from an oppressed creature to a free one.[4] Later in her development, Rich might not use "beautiful as any boy" to describe this transformation, but in the context of this volume the male imagery can be regarded as an element of a pattern we are fully prepared for by earlier poems and by earlier sections in "Snapshots." In essence, this pattern treats women's selves as costumes and women's costumes as selves.

Section 9, for example, takes as its starting point an allusion to Samuel Johnson's remark about a woman's preaching:

> *Not that it is done well, but*
> *that it is done at all?* Yes, think
> of the odds! or shrug them off forever.
> This luxury of the precocious child,
> Time's precious chronic invalid,—
> would we, darlings, resign it if we could?
> Our blight has been our sinecure:
> mere talent was enough for us—
> glitter in fragments and rough drafts.

The opening question about woman's achievement in the public sector brings on the flippant: "Yes, think / of the odds! or shrug them off forever." The speaker's tone then becomes more biting as she refers to woman as "Time's precious chronic invalid." Rich scolds, but does not excuse herself from the same failings: "mere talent was enough for us." Sarcastic and witty, she proceeds:

> Sigh no more, ladies.
> 　　　　　　Time is male
> and in his cups drinks to the fair.
> Bemused by gallantry, we hear
> our mediocrities over-praised,
> indolence read as abnegation,
> slattern thought styled intuition,
> every lapse forgiven, our crime
> only to cast too bold a shadow
> or smash the mold straight off.

The last two lines temper the sarcasm somewhat. The first admits that a woman can achieve a largeness of stature, even though this might be perceived as a crime. Perhaps more compelling is the other alternative: to "smash the mold straight off." A provocative image, it suggests that a woman need not be confined to that category "woman"—that the distinction of gender is a shell or a costume which can be discarded. The radical act of breaking the "mold" of gender threatens the social order and "For that, solitary confinement / tear gas, attrition shelling. / Few applicants for that honor." While Rich understands the risks involved in breaking out of the bounds of gender, she is relentless and her tone has a cutting edge.

In another section, she presents an image of a traditional "feminine" woman as seen through a feminist eye. Taking the first line of a poem by Thomas Campion, she constructs a biting, but mellifluous parody:

> When to her lute Corinna sings
> neither words nor music are her own;
> only the long hair dipping
> over her cheek, only the song
> of silk against her knees
> and these
> adjusted in reflections of an eye.

While the music Corinna plays and sings may be another's composition, her hair is her own as is "the song / of silk against her knees." Thus Rich emphasizes elements of the woman musician's costume. Because Corinna aims to please—and not to create—her costume becomes the essence of her self, something "adjusted in reflections of an eye." In a similar fashion, Antinoüs describes "What I've swallowed from glasses, eyes, motions of hands." As in the Antinoüs poem, Rich treats costume with wit, particularly in the play on words: "the song / of silk against her knees." Rich's tone becomes significant when it is seen as an element in her lack of conservatism about sex roles and "properly sexed" clothing.

Being clothed in a womanly, seductive fashion only serves to trap Corinna. While "the song of silk" is her own, the words and music are not. Thus she becomes merely a mimic and a flirt. Within this passage, Rich's tone mocks heterosexual flirtation. There is no logical reason why seductive clothing or the act of performing someone else's music should necessarily lead to the emptiness and artificiality that Rich derides. If, however, the clothing and behavior constitute a substitution for a developed selfhood, then Rich convinces. The only "right action" then becomes to throw the clothing away. This poem does not pursue this line of thought to its logical outcome—nakedness. Instead, Rich's imagination moves in the second part of the Corinna section toward a characteristic type of female imagery:[5]

> Poised, trembling and unsatisfied, before
> an unlocked door, that cage of cages,
> tell us, you bird, you tragical machine—
> is this *fertilisante douleur?*

Rich imagines woman as a bird in an unlocked cage rather than the naked self free of its false costume. Herein lies a key difference between the male and female modernist.

For Rich, as for the female modernists cited by Gilbert, the naked self is no more true than the costumed self. Perhaps the reason lies in the use or the misuse of the female body, particularly in modern times. In advertisements, in pornography, a woman's nakedness serves purposes not necessarily her own. In her bird metaphor, Rich signifies a different perception of the "reality" of gender as well as a rejection of the polarities so central to the male modernists' handling of similar material. Aside from the cagedness and the delicacy of the bird, it ultimately signifies both flight and freedom from oppression. In this section, the bird—the woman—does not fly away, though its cage is unlocked. Woman's oppression, Rich implies, is sweetened by her status. She concludes:

> Pinned down
> by love, for you the only natural action,
> are you edged more keen
> to prise the secrets of the vault?

Rich's tone is ambivalent about a woman's loving relationship with others. While they "pin her down," they may also constitute a special power. A new idea emerges: "has Nature shown / her household books to you, daughter-in-law, / that her sons never saw?" In her questions, Rich goes beyond the rhetorical to the heart of one of her most compelling concerns. Beyond anatomy, beyond their special spheres of influence, what is the difference between men and women? Has Nature granted woman a special power? The image patterns in this poem and the male identification seen in other poems suggest answers that transcend the truth of gender.

The last poem in the volume, "The Roofwalker" (1961), carries a dedication to Denise Levertov and brings these themes to their culmination, both in terms of its male identification and in its treatment of the naked self. The poem begins as a straightforward description with existential overtones of a group of roofers finishing up their work as night falls:

> Giants, the roofwalkers,
> on a listing deck, the wave
> of darkness about to break
> on their heads.

After this opening, which sets the scene and the metaphorical basis for the poem, the first-person pronoun enters and the poem takes an imaginative leap in seeing a connection between the external event and the speaker's state of mind:

> I feel like them up there:
> exposed, larger than life,
> and due to break my neck.
>
> Was it worth while to lay—
> with infinite exertion—
> a roof I can't live under?
> —All those blueprints,
> closings of gaps,
> measurings, calculations?
> A life I didn't choose
> chose me: even

my tools are the wrong ones
for what I have to do.
I'm naked, ignorant,
a naked man fleeing
across the roofs
who could with a shade of difference
be sitting in the lamplight
against the cream wallpaper
reading—not with indifference—
about a naked man
fleeing across the roofs.

The clear, unequivocal statement of feeling at the center of the poem operates as a pivot, turning the poem from its opening description to its metaphysical third section. There is an *emotional* nakedness to the lines, a baring of the self that is, at the same time, not confessional. The last section takes its structure from the roof metaphor and advances in two motions. In the first, the speaker uses the roof to represent the way she has constructed her life. Even with all her care, "A life I didn't choose, / chose me." The poet expresses here a kind of truism about "the best-laid plans" which often go awry. The second movement of this part ("I'm a naked man") throws the poem beyond truism into a radical perspective. Perhaps Rich chose the male identification because it seemed in keeping with the actual roofers with whom she began. We can assume they were male, female construction workers being uncommon in 1961. We might also see "The Roofwalker" as another of Rich's animus poems in which the risks she takes are aspects of her journey into the self.

Rich's attitude toward the changeability of the self suggests an alternative reading that this chapter has been building toward. With irony and ambiguity, the speaker identifies herself as "a naked man fleeing / across the roofs" and at the same time as a man "sitting in the lamplight / . . . reading—not with indifference— / about a naked man / fleeing across the roofs." She could be either; the changeable selves signify both the uncertainty of the transitional state and the concept of transvestism as metaphor. Most likely, the restrictions imposed on her gender compose an element of those societal terms Rich rejects. Thus Rich's projection of her female persona into alternative male figures adds further evidence to a concept of a gender-free reality where selves are costumes and costumes are selves. Nakedness is thus another costume, worn for a while perhaps, definitely reckless in the context of this poem, but "with a shade of difference," changeable. In this poem, the sense of flux challenges "truths" about the nature of the self and gender; hence we get that heightened sense of vulnerability Rich expresses. "An age of changing clothes," as Susan Gilbert says, offers "vertiginous freedom"— and anxiety. How much more anxious an age like ours when the truths of gender are being shaken to the roots, especially by Adrienne Rich.

The factors that would lead Rich to explore accepted truths about gender reality and its supposed fixity can be deduced from her life story and her poetic career as well as from a climate of change which would culminate in the human rights movements of the sixties. Rich had a close relationship with her father, and she writes about this as a key influence in her development as a writer and as a particular kind of woman: "My own luck was being born white and middle-class into a house full of books, with a father who encouraged me to read and write. So for about twenty years I wrote for a particular man, who criticized and praised me and made me feel I was indeed 'special'" (ARP, p. 93). She grew into a "special" woman, but her specialness was always defined by males—her father, other writers, teachers—including, one supposes, her husband. As Rich points out about herself and other women like her, "we have known that men would tolerate, even romanticize us as special, as long as our words and actions didn't threaten their privilege of tolerating or rejecting us according to their ideas of what a special woman ought to be" (p. 93). Thus we see the hold that male approval had upon her psyche, a hold that she deeply resented.

To give up that approval, however, would put her at great risk, as "The Roofwalker" shows. In rejecting this life she did not choose, the speaker in Rich's poem also finds her tools lacking: "even my tools are the wrong ones / for what I have to do."

Tools can be read as the techniques of her poetic craft, the metaphor from "The Diamond Cutters." "Respect the adversary," she writes, "Meet it with tools refined." Although her tools may not be the right ones, she does not abandon them: witness the craft of this poem—from the brillance of her extended metaphor to the steady control of the iambic trimeters. Such craft allows her to handle, with great competence, a poem about the mind at risk—and it does not abandon her, though she may belittle it. Rich's dedication to her sister poet Denise Levertov provides a clue to the new strategy she will need to employ in resolving the anxiety of the transitional state. In effect, she creates for herself the female alliance that she needs, for "The Roofwalker" does not remain sitting in the protection of the patriarchal living room.

In this context, then, the turmoil of "The Roofwalker" is the motivation that will lead Adrienne Rich to define herself on her own terms and in alliance with other women. Though Rich may identify with men in this volume, she no longer worships maleness as power. Her portrayal of women, however, stresses the power-to-transform. She herself has displayed that power through her use of transvestism as metaphor. If women's power-to-transform is cultivated outside the sphere of male influence, *Snapshots* implies, the emergence of a truly different creature occurs, one unimpeded by the constraints of gender. Rich gives a glimpse of this new creature as she "plunges / breasted and glancing through the currents." A new poetry is beginning here, one that is distinctively female in nature and forged in women's experience and perceptions.

The subtext of this volume is the poet's desire to free herself from her earlier poetic mentors, most of whom were male. Thus complicated issues of sexuality and creativity arise. In order to develop as a poet—or as any other kind of artist—one must go through a process of being influenced and then throwing off those influences.[6] To be influenced too much by other poets smothers the individual creative spirit. Thus the poet must struggle for artistic survival. When the poet is a woman influenced by male poets, as was Rich, the struggle to gain breathing space for one's own creativity could turn into a sexual conflict and provide further evidence of patriarchal oppression of female energies. Until women artists engage in the influence struggle with other women artists, something that is bound to happen in the next generation, we will be unable to accurately assess the dimensions of the struggle for female artistic identity in poets such as Rich. For the time being, however, we can understand how her struggle to free herself from male poetic influences also made her acutely sensitive to male domination in the social and political spheres.

CHAPTER 5

MORE THAN
A SYMPTOM:
*NECESSITIES
OF LIFE*
(1966)

PRIMARY among the "necessities of life" in Adrienne Rich's fourth book of poetry is language. By language, I mean the capacity for speech from the self. In *Silences,* Tillie Olsen describes this form of expression as discoverable in places not usually considered "art": "the journal, letters, memoirs, personal utterances—for they come more natural for most, closer to possibility of use, of shaping—and, *in one's own words,* become source, add to the authentic store of human life, human experience" (italics in original).[1] Olsen's emphasis upon usefulness, individual expression, and the enlargement of experience captures the sense in which Adrienne Rich deems language a necessity of life.

In some poems, Rich defines the quality of this language negatively; she explores what it should not be. Certain contexts, images and collocations of words create these negative definitions. In other poems, she moves toward a positive definition, implying that this language *as story* can accomplish what Rich's speaker accomplishes in her title poem: rebirth and the widening of possibility. Furthermore, she suggests that such a language may well be uttered by a woman. Necessary language is woman's "unsaid word"—her withheld speech—transformed. In this conversion, the will plays a decisive role. In effect, poems such as those in *Necessities of Life* will eventually lead Rich in 1979 to articulate a position about women, language, and power: "When we become acutely, disturbingly aware of the language we are using and that is using us, we begin to grasp a material resource that women have never before collectively attemptd to repossess (though we were its inventors, and though individual writers like Dickinson, Woolf, Stein, H.D., have approached language as transforming power)" (*On Lies, Secrets, and Silence*, p. 247). In insisting upon language as a necessity of life Rich initiates her movement toward the later declaration.

In "An Unsaid Word" from her first volume of poetry, Rich's persona willed not to speak, thus enabling her man to wander in his "estranged intensity." In her fourth volume of poems, her personas continue such willfulness, but their purposes differ. More aware of the power of language, some speakers withhold their words in order to create more lively possibilities for themselves and others. The essence of that liveliness is the rebirth or renewal that characterizes transformation. Counterposed against the power-to-control, transforming power inheres in language that is authentic, useful, and life-enhancing.

Two women poets, Emily Dickinson and Sylvia Plath, are part of Adrienne Rich's discoveries about language. The quality of their lives and / or their language enters the texture of Rich's *Necessities of Life*, her most accomplished book of poems so far. Dickinson, for example, appears in a poem that takes its title from a line in one of Dickinson's letters—"I am in Danger— Sir—." She provides Adrienne Rich with a model of a woman who has "it out at last / on [her] own premises." Language, for Dickinson, was a necessity of life, as it is for Adrienne Rich. The contemporary poet Sylvia Plath also appeals to Rich's poetic consciousness, but Plath's influence was only temporary. At this stage, it is important simply to recognize that Rich turns to women poets where previously she had consciously imitated men. Her attraction to women poets signifies the importance for Rich of the formation of a female aesthetic. She can become the poet she is destined to be once she yokes her identity as poet-woman or woman-poet. In turning to other poets who share the issues of female identity and creativity, Rich attends to her art and envisions a new (for her) synthesis of identity. Integral to the unity of poet and woman is language. *Necessities of Life* brings Adrienne Rich closer to an understanding of the nature of that language and its purpose.

Rich begins the volume with her title poem, an exultant yet ironic declaration about rebirth and identity in the early post-modernist mode. Abandoning the modernist prescription against "the personal" in poetry, Rich adopts the first-person singular pronoun, but the "I" still functions as a mask. While we can assume an autobiographical self-exploration, the speaker's objective, almost clinical tone defies the "confessional" mode. Although she never identifies herself as a woman, the image patterns betray a female mind at work.

In the first section of the poem, the speaker describes her birth in painterly images: "a hard little head protruding / from the pointillist's buzz and bloom." Passive and malleable, the speaker comes under a variety of influences: "I was Wittgenstein, / Mary Wollstonecraft, the soul / of Louis Jouvet." The poem turns as the speaker insists on shaping her own nature:

> Till, wolfed almost to shreds,
> I learned to make myself
>
> unappetizing. Scaly as a dry bulb
> thrown into a cellar
>
> I used myself, let nothing use me.
> Like being on a private dole,
>
> sometimes more like kneading bricks in Egypt.
> What life was there, was mine,
>
> now and again to lay
> one hand on a warm brick
>
> and touch the sun's ghost
> with economical joy,
>
> now and again to name
> over the bare necessities.

So much for those days. Soon
practice may make me middling-perfect, I'll

dare inhabit the world
trenchant in motion as an eel, solid

as a cabbage-head. I have invitations:
a curl of mist steams upward

from a field, visible as my breath,
houses along a road stand waiting

like old women knitting, breathless
to tell their tales.

(1962)

Judith Gardiner's definition of "female identity as a process" helps us to understand the dynamics of the poem. Gardiner sees "female identity as typically less fixed, less unitary, and more flexible than male individuality, both in its primary core and in the entire maturational complex developed from this core. "These traits," says Gardiner, "have far-reaching consequences for the distinctive nature of writing by women" (*Writing and Sexual Difference,* p. 183). Rich's poem provides a striking example of Gardiner's theory, for the speaker sees herself going through various shapes, sizes, colors, and biographies until she calls a halt to the whole process and takes charge of her own rebirth. "Unappetizing" becomes a key word and works in conjunction with the image "scaly as a dry bulb." In other words, she makes herself ugly; no more biographies are going to come and swallow her up. Now for a woman to make herself ugly— even the masked woman in the poem—is to violate one of the cardinal rules of female social behavior. Nonetheless, Rich refuses to create an "appropriate" womanly image for herself.

Her act is radical, as Judith Gardiner points out: "Women are encouraged to judge their inner selves through their external physical appearance and to equate the two. At the same time, they are taught to create socially approved images of themselves by manipulating their dress, speech, and behavior" (p. 190).

What Rich's speaker does when she makes herself "unappetizing" and "scaly" is to ignore those socially dictated norms. This act results in no dire consequences; in fact, it brings about a moment of intense awareness of the little pleasures of life: "now again to lay / one hand on a warm brick / and touch the sun's ghost / with economical joy." The speaker refuses to take herself or this moment too seriously and the ending of the poem backs away from any sense of exultance or superiority. The images border on the self-effacing and comical: "practice may make me middling-perfect," "trenchant in motion as an eel," "solid as a cabbage-head." Even the smug "I have invitations" turns out to be slightly ironic. No one has invited her anywhere because of her new and better self; her perceptions, however, are inviting: "a curl of mist," those "houses" described as "waiting / like old women knitting, breathless / to tell their tales." If these last lines are intended to offer closure to the poem, they are enigmatic.

How are we supposed to read them? Women are mentioned for the first time and that is significant, one supposes, but almost offhand. They are *old* women, which completes the cycle of birth, youth, rebirth, and maturity. Perhaps they are "breathless to tell their tales" as the speaker has been eager to tell us *her* story. Perhaps this is the implied theme of the poem: that a woman who tells her own tale creates her own biography; she bestows an identity on herself. Thus among the "necessities of life" is language, as essential, one might surmise, as breathing.

Venturing closer to the personal, "In the Woods" (1963) gives us a speaker who is a writer, a woman, and someone who alludes both to other people's poetry (in this case, to that of the Dutch poet J. C. Bloem, the source of Rich's first line) and to an image from a poem by Rich.[2] Forging a closer connection between the speaker and the poet, "In the Woods" gives us a Whitmanesque, transcendental experience couched in distinctly unRomantic terms.

The first section of the poem proceeds from the statement of a thesis into its dramatic enactment, the interior monologue of a person in the process of self-discovery:

"Difficult ordinary happiness,"
no one nowadays believes in you.
I shift, full-length on the blanket,
to fix the sun precisely

behind the pine-tree's crest
so light spreads through the needles
alive as water just
where a snake has surfaced,

unreal as water in green crystal.
Bad news is always arriving.
"We're hiders, hiding from something bad,"
sings the little boy.

Writing these words in the woods,
I feel like a traitor to my friends,
even to my enemies.
The common lot's to die

a stranger's death and lie
rouged in the coffin, in a dress
chosen by the funeral director.
Perhaps that's why we never

see clocks on public buildings any more.
A fact no architect will mention.
We're hiders, hiding from something bad
most of the time.

As the speaker's thoughts shift from the general disbelief in "difficult ordinary happiness" to her own presence in a natural setting, she reprimands herself. Who is she, after all, to separate herself from others and make pronouncements? "I feel like a traitor to my friends, / even to my enemies," she says. She may be too happy. Or her alienation may stem from the act of writing. To bring herself back to "the common lot," she thinks about death, specifically of a dead woman: "rouged in the coffin, in a dress / chosen by the funeral director." Although oblique, Rich's image of the dead woman is her closest female identification. In addition, she admits she is among the "hiders, hiding from something bad" here in the woods. This second mentioning of the hiders is not in quotation marks: the speaker reduces her distance from the reader. But not for long.

The remainder of the poem concerns a transcendental moment:

> Yet, and outrageously, something good
> finds us, found me this morning
> lying on a dusty blanket
> among the burnt-out Indian pipes
>
> and bursting-open lady's-slippers.
> My soul, my helicopter, whirred
> distantly, by habit, over
> the old pond with the half-drowned boat
>
> toward which it always veers
> for consolation: ego's Arcady:
> leaving the body stuck
> like a leaf against a screen.—
>
> Happiness! how many times
> I've stranded on that word,
> at the edge of that pond; seen
> as if through tears, the dragon-fly—
>
> only to find it all
> going differently for once
> this time: my soul wheeled back
> and burst into my body.
>
> Found! Ready or not.
> If I move now, the sun
> naked between the trees
> will melt me as I lie.

Rich anchors her transcendence in graphic, earthy terms: "lying on a dusty blanket / among the burnt-out Indian pipes." The speaker believes in "difficult ordinary happiness" almost in spite of her deliberate attempt not to. As in the game of hide and seek, the speaker is "Found! ready or not." Thus even at the moment of illumination about the unity of body and soul, the speaker, with a touch of humor, makes her joy human, accessible, and the product of "leaning and loafing," perhaps even "inviting my soul." The echoes of Whitman's "Song of Myself" are subtle and entirely plausible since the poem immediately following "In the Woods" contains an epigraph from Whitman.

Through its self-effacing tone, the poem extends itself to include "the common lot," those who may never approach illumination or the poet's posture as that special person who achieves transcendence and issues a communiqué. Rich would like to have it both ways: to be the poet, the namer of these special, "ordinary" experiences, and to be one of those who find it difficult to believe in "ordinary happiness." These needs reflect Rich's awareness of her growing strength as a poet and the conflict this arouses with her self-concept as a woman. To be a poet, to set herself apart, "in the woods" or elsewhere goes contrary to the traditional sense of a woman's role. As Gardiner makes clear in her study of women writers, "Often they communicate a consciousness of their identity through paradoxes of sameness and difference—from other women, especially their mothers; from men; and from social injunctions for what women should be, including those inscribed in the literary canon" (*Writing and Sexual Difference*, p. 184). "In the Woods" bounces back and forth in paradoxical fashion, although not in the strict categories Gardiner mentions. The paradoxes intertwine and circle back upon one another: Rich is the same as other people, yet different. She is a poet. Like all poets she can communicate those truths that lie beyond the ordinary ken. Yet she is different from most poets because she is a woman; and she differs from most women because she is a poet. The contrariness of these differences make up Rich's identity.

In "The Corpse-Plant," a companion piece to "In the Woods," the paradoxes diminish and Rich claims a destiny for herself tied to her sense of the poet as namer and as woman. She uses a question asked by Walt Whitman as an epigraph: "How can an obedient man, or a sick man, dare to write poems?" A contemplative response to this question occupies the speaker as she sits inside at night staring at some "corpse-plants / clustered in a hobnailed tumbler." As she studies the plants she picked in the

74

woods that day, she recalls Whitman's question and answers it, adding her own twist:

> Neither obedient nor sick, I turn my head,
> feeling the weight of a thick gold ring
> in either lobe. I see the corpse-plants
> clustered in a hobnailed tumbler.

"Neither obedient nor sick"—nor a man—the speaker dares to write poems. The first two terms are stated as abstractions; the third enters the poem obliquely in the image of the speaker's earrings. Through them she implicitly defines herself as a woman. In the center of the poem, the speaker goes into greater detail about her earrings, developing in the process her sense of connection through time and history with another woman:

> The gold in my ears,
> souvenir of a shrewd old city,
> might have been wearing thin as wires
> found in the bones of a woman's head
>
> miraculously kept in its essentials
> in some hot cradle-tomb of time.
> I felt my body slipping through
> the fingers of its mind.

The last two lines reiterate the mystical experience in the woods of the previous poem. Significantly, Rich's speaker retains from that experience something concrete—the corpse-plants. In the remainder of the poem she elaborates upon the corpse-plants, defining them as symbols and telling how they received their name. Common Indian pipes, the corpse-plants attain the status of icons.

Earlier in the poem Rich had identified her speaker as a woman;now she emerges as a poet or namer: "I gave them their deathly names— / or did they name themselves?— / not 'Indian pipes' as once / we children knew them." The exploratory nature of this section exemplifies Rich's attitude toward language. First she names them, then she questions where they got their name.

Whatever its origin, "corpse-plant" is more mature than "Indian pipes" since that was how the speaker "knew them" as a child when she accepted names as givens. Her adult naming is a personal act that is *useful* to her. As icons or objects of meditation, the plants bring Rich's speaker to thoughts of her mortality: "winters of mind, of flesh, / sickness of the rot-smell of leaves." The point is that she *chooses* to generate such thoughts. Rich's speaker is a woman, a poet, and willful: "Only death's insect whiteness / crooks its neck in a tumbler / where I placed its sign *by choice*." Out of that willfulness comes her power to create her own reality. She could easily, passively have accepted transcendence. Along with the ease of achieving such an existence, Rich rejects the sense of being above "the common lot," which is "to die," as she says in her previous poem. Her sensibility prompts her return to a contemplation of "the common lot," not because she is obedient or sick but because she is a poet with a "dream of a common language" that she barely glimpses in *Necessities of Life*. Central to any language she will articulate is the nature of its speaker. She is starting to realize that she must embrace not just "the common lot" of mortality but her own womanhood. While countless poets dwell on the theme of mortality, defining the poet as woman is the unique contribution of Adrienne Rich. This does not, of course, strip man of his poetic mantle, just his exclusive possession of it. Rich also challenges the notion that a Sappho or an Emily Dickinson is a magnificent exception in a predominantly male literary canon.

Adrienne Rich is not the only modern writer to insist upon a special awareness of female artistic creativity. She is, however, the most visible and prominent poet in the last half of the twentieth century to take as her primary objective the creation and promotion of a female aesthetic. Rich may be compared to Virginia Woolf who, in *A Room of One's Own*, declares that woman's "creative power" is unique and different from man's:

And one must conclude that it would be a thousand pities if [woman's creative power] were hindered or wasted, for it was won by centuries of the most drastic discipline, and there is nothing to take its place. It would be a thousand pities if women wrote like men, or lived like men, or looked like men, for if two sexes are quite inadequate, considering the vastness and variety of the world, how should we manage with one only?[3]

Virginia Woolf cultivated that difference in her novels, as Rich does in her poems. *Necessities of Life* provides the opportunity to observe the poet's growing awareness that being a woman is an essential aspect of her unique creative power. Thus we see the significance of the poet's adoption of a female persona who shapes language by choosing her own signs, naming her own names.

Up to this point in the volume, Rich's speakers have been alone; their essential action has been reflection and/or meditation. As Rich becomes more capable of imagining a listener in her poetry and of bringing that listener into her poetic structures, her focus on language becomes charged with immediacy. "Like This Together" deals with a marital relationship and is an amazingly naked poem for Rich; here the poet's life appears to flow into her poetry and the issues she has been grappling with in her poems help her to reorder her life. In a statement made at a poetry reading in 1964, the year after this poem, Rich puts this process into her own words: "instead of poems about experience, I am getting poems that are experiences, that contribute to my knowledge and my emotional life even while they reflect and assimilate it" (*ARP*, p. 89). "Like This Together" is such a poem.

The five parts of this lengthy poem appear as seemingly disconnected fragments. The urban setting unifies the poem as does Rich's highly developed sense of the natural world. The poem's imagery flows between those two worlds. Its drama is the possibility of connection, its urgency the need to transform a marriage. Urban and natural are connected; people are connected: "like this together." For the most part, it is a bad connection and static ensues. Rich explores how inadequate language creates disruptive friction. Ultimately, the poem moves from clutched silence to clear speech; its way is cluttered with ruined language: buzz words, clichés, misnomers. The quest is for words that understand or "fit" us so that transformation can occur.

The speaker of the poem is a woman. Strong-willed, she corrects, speaks, and at times remains silent. In each of these actions, her will to choose plays a key role. We recognize, for example, the willfulness of the unsaid word in part 1:

> Wind rocks the car.
> We sit parked by the river,
> silence between our teeth.
> Birds scatter across islands
> of broken ice. Another time
> I'd have said: "Canada geese,"
> knowing you love them.

While both are silent, the woman makes an explicit refusal of certain words. She will not say what she knows will please her husband. "Canada geese" is a buzz word; press it or say it and get a known reaction: a smile? delight? The unsaid word in this context refuses to maintain the status quo of a relationship that has brought the two people to the iced-over river where they sit "like drugged birds / in a glass case." Negative in its denial of language and in its metaphor of half-alive birds, the first section establishes the poem's direction: what kind of communication could revivify the marriage?

Part 3 ventures an answer by taking a cliché and turning it around. The woman says to her husband, "We have, as they say, / certain things in common." This cliché does not beget more of the same: we laugh at the same jokes, love the same foods, prefer the ocean to the mountains. Instead, the speaker details the ordinary, intimate texture of their life together: "I mean: a view / from a bathroom window / . . . the way / water tastes from our tap." In the act of renewing the cliché with her own meaning— *their* own meaning—the speaker moves closer to what connects them, what they do, indeed, have "in common." This sense, then, of what is common and of value ("the taste of water, / a luxury I might / otherwise have missed") emerges out of a transformed cliché.

Water is "a luxury." "You (the husband) are my mother." The speaker of this poem thinks about such namings-that-misname and says, "Our words misunderstand us." This serious charge dominates the fourth section of the poem, a section that comes closer to understanding why they are "like this together"— that is, "like drugged birds / in a glass case." Along with telling her husband that "sometimes at night / you are my mother," she names him "my cave" and "the wave of birth / that drowns me in my first / nightmare." Mother, cave, wave of birth: these three terms have mythic overtones of psychic rebirth. The old myths, however, do not work. Nor the old names. He is *not* her mother. She must become her own mother. She must find new names, new relationships, for the consequences of maintaining the usual misnomers are severe. Instead of rebirth, there is abortion: "Miscarried knowledge twists us / like hot sheets thrown askew." In this context, to miscarry means to go astray, to be lost in transition. The speaker does not want this; she longs for transformation. The final stanza asserts this goal for *both* of them:

> Dead winter doesn't die,
> it wears away, a piece of carrion
> picked clean at last,
> rained away or burnt dry.
> Our desiring does this,
> make no mistake, I'm speaking
> of fact: through mere indifference
> we could prevent it.
> Only our fierce attention
> gets hyacinths out of those
> hard cerebral lumps,
> unwraps the wet buds down
> the whole length of a stem.

Is this ending "forced" as Helen Vendler says? She finds Rich off-base in her declaration "that love can be kept alive by our work-ing at it, that the dry scaly bulb can be pried into life" (*ARP*, p. 168). There *is* a forcefulness to the ending, an insistence upon the speaker's position that seems inflexible, possibly unattractive in a woman. The language is blunt and to the point, the meta-phors brilliant. Where she would not speak before, she speaks now. Out of her unsaid word, her denial of spoiled language, comes her power: "I'm *speaking* of fact." No more silence, but utterance whose goal is transformation. In the speaker's view, "dead winter" does not simply turn into spring. If winter has to be acted upon by spring rains, why not, then, a relationship come to impasse? The will plays its part—"only our fierce attention / gets hyacinths out of those / hard cerebral lumps"—and the poem concludes with a flowering where there was none, a vision of the kind of attention that will bring renewal. As the poem attests, attention to language is integral to that transformation, thus a necessity of life.

In her autobiographical essay "When We Dead Awaken," Rich describes transforming power as a basic function for writers in general; for women writers, however, it constitutes a dilemma:

> If the imagination is to transcend and transform experience it has to question, to challenge, to conceive of alternatives, perhaps to the very life you are living at that moment. You have to be free to play around with the notion that day might be night, love might be hate; nothing can be too sacred for the imagination to turn into its opposite or to call experimentally by another name. For writing is re-naming. Now, to be maternally with small children in the old way, to be with a man in the old way of marriage, requires a holding-back, a putting-aside of that imaginative activity, and seems to demand instead a kind of conservatism. I want to make it clear that I am *not* saying that in order to write well, or think well, it is necessary to become unavailable to others, or to become a devouring ego. This has been the myth of the masculine artist and thinker; and I repeat, I do not accept it. But to be a female human being trying to fulfill traditional female functions in a traditional way *is* in direct conflict with the subversive function of the imagination. The word traditional is important here. There must be ways, and we will be finding out more and more about them, in which the energy of creation and the energy of relation can be united. (*ARP*, p. 96)

Thus Rich's aesthetic direction (the energy of creation) becomes a personal and emotional direction (the energy of relation). What she desires for her poetry she desires as well in her personal relationships—and for other women. In all instances, language holds the key to transforming power.

Rich's poem about Emily Dickinson brings these patterns of meanings to a culmination. "I am in Danger—Sir—" does not name Dickinson as the subject; she has named herself despite being called "half-cracked" by Higginson (or his wife) or becoming "famous in garbled versions." The poem moves from Higginson's misnomer and the public's misapprehension into an analysis of the relationship between language and the poet. Rich imagines Emily Dickinson's retreat from the world as being caused by an intense focus on language, as if Dickinson literally could not live with the "spoiled language" about her and had to withdraw to a world shaped and sustained, the poem implies, by the language of her poetry:

> you, woman, masculine
> in single-mindedness,
> for whom the word was more
> than a symptom—
>
> a condition of being.
> Till the air buzzing with spoiled language
> sang in your ears
> of Perjury
>
> and in your half-cracked way you chose
> silence for entertainment,
> chose to have it out at last
> on your own premises.

In several ways this poem manifests Rich's chief concerns in this volume. First, it names language as a necessity of life for Dickinson: "a condition of being." Second, it affirms Rich's criticism of words that *misunderstand:* "spoiled language / sang in your ears / of Perjury." Third, it regards silence as a viable choice given the conditions. Of course, Emily Dickinson's silence was not dumb. Silence, therefore, was both preferable to "spoiled language" and the generator of poems; out of silence, the word. Finally, Rich's elegant pun in the last line emphasizes the role of the will:

Dickinson "*chose* to have it out at last / on [her] own premises."
Yet Rich terms Dickinson's vocation "masculine / in single-
mindedness." Masculinity is power—so the poem says. Dickinson's act in "having it out . . . / on [her] own premises" em-
powered her.

Rich's essay on Emily Dickinson sheds some light on the re-
tention of masculine in this poem. "Vesuvius at Home" is sub-
titled "The Power of Emily Dickinson." In it, Rich studies
Dickinson's use of masculine pronouns and posits how these
pronouns "can refer simultaneously to many aspects of the
'masculine' in the patriarchal world—the god she engages in
dialogue, again on *her* terms; her own creative powers, unsexing
for a woman, the male power-figures in her immediate
environment."[4]

In each of these three suggestions, power is linked to maleness. God embodies the supreme (masculine) power; creative
powers are deemed masculine; "power-figures" in Dickinson's
life were men. Rich's hypothesis suggests that imagining any
other way of defining power was difficult, if not impossible, for
Emily Dickinson. In *Necessities of Life* the same holds true for
Adrienne Rich. Barbara Grizzuti Harrison, in a *New Republic*
review of *On Lies, Secrets, and Silence* in which this essay is
collected, finds Rich's reading of Dickinson's poems "eccentric."
She quotes Rich as saying, "they are about the poet's relationship to her own power, which is exteriorized in masculine
form." To Harrison, Rich appears "a polemicist" in these remarks (and elsewhere), "her respect and love for the written
word betrayed by her ideology."[5] There is no denying that Rich
becomes an ideologue of the women's revolution, nor that her
assessment of Dickinson's poetry reflects her feminist ideology.
Does this mean that her reflections on Dickinson must be dismissed? A woman's relationship to power and power-figures is a
central fact of her existence. Rich challenges us to consider that
relationship.

In her fourth book of poems, Rich makes some implicit connections between woman, the poet, and power. The poem "I am
in Danger—Sir—" brings her to the recognition that Emily

Dickinson's power as a poet emerged out of a desperate struggle for self-definition, an aspect of which was her right to use language in her own way. Clearly Rich's own struggles as a poet enter this poem and she projects onto Dickinson her own concerns. The most explicit connection between Dickinson and Rich consists in how they both—for a while at least—"chose silence for entertainment." Rich's "silence" took the form of subterfuge, subversion of her male models or the use of womanly silence as a motif in her poems. In her Dickinson essay, Rich identifies herself with her female predecessor. "As a woman poet finding my own methods," she says, "I have come to understand [Emily Dickinson's] necessities, could have been witness in her defense."[6] Primary among those necessities was a language that was not "spoiled."

In her quest for such a language, Rich turns to the poetry of Sylvia Plath, a sign that she is looking, among other things, toward another woman poet for intimations of what that language might be. Several poems in the volume show Plath's influence; among these are "The Knot," "Side By Side," and "Not Like That," where it is most apparent.

Sylvia Plath's "Tulips" (1962) and Adrienne Rich's "Not Like That" (1965) both treat the subject of death.[7] Rich has written other poems in *Necessities of Life* that also concern this subject: "After Dark" about the death of her father; "Mourning Picture" about a painting by Edwin Romanzo Elmer that depicts his and his wife's mourning for their child; "Halfway" about the death of Rich's grandmother; and, of course, "The Corpse-Plant." Thus her poem "Not Like That" emerges from Rich's sustained involvement with the subject. Certain phrases, however, appear to be culled from several of Plath's poems. In general, Rich's attempt to achieve some of Plath's startling effects is unfortunate. A comparison of the two poems will indicate how, and perhaps why, Rich was unsuccessful.

"Tulips" takes place in a hospital where the speaker is recovering from an operation. She regards some red tulips that have been sent her, resenting their flamboyant proclamation of life: "The tulips are too red in the first place, they hurt me." She prefers a numbness close to death, and the poem's hospital environment is transformed into the world of death: "Look how white everything is, how quiet, how snowed-in. / I am learning peacefulness, lying by myself quietly." In a similar fashion, Rich takes as her setting another world of death—a cemetery. Unlike Plath, Rich creates a distance between her speaker and the world of death by making the experience one enacted by children—not specific children, just "The children love to play up here." Where Plath transforms the hospital room into a death chamber, "Not Like That" begins in one—the cemetery. What the poems have in common is a desire to discard life. Plath's speaker wants only:

> To lie with my hands turned up and be utterly empty.
> how free it is, you have no idea how free—
> The peacefulness is so big it dazes you
> . . . .
> It is what the dead close on, finally; I imagine them
> shutting their mouths on it, like a communion tablet.

Similarly, Rich's speaker describes what the children like to do in the cemetery:

> It's so pure in the cemetery,
> the children love to play up here.
> It's a little town, a game of blocks,
> a village packed in a box,
> a pre-war German toy.
> . . . .
> To come and sit here forever,
> a cup of tea in one's lap
> and one's eyes closed lightly, lightly,
> perfectly still
> in a nineteenth-century sleep!
> it seems so natural to die.

Plathlike phrases enter the first stanza, although some are not directly from "Tulips." Rich's phrase, "a pre-war German toy," for example, calls to mind the many references to Germany in Plath's poems ("Daddy," "The Munich Mannequins," and "Little Fugue"). Rich's reference to *German* seems gratuitous because, unlike Plath, she does not have available to her the richness of connotation built up over a number of poems. As for Rich's "it seems so normal to die," this is what "Tulips" affirms, but does not say directly. Elsewhere, in "Lady Lazarus," for example, Plath captures a similar detachment in "Dying is an art, like everything else. / I do it exceptionally well." In truth, however, Rich's lines seem a distillation of the general tone of many of Plath's poems rather than a specific borrowing.

The closest direct link between the two poems is the word *pure*. Rich opens with "It's so pure in the cemetery." In "Tulips," Sylvia Plath writes, "I have never been so pure." *Pure* is a code word for Plath, part of the ritual of transformation: the cleansing necessary for rebirth. It has no special significance for Rich.

While the similarities in tone and some phrasing may connect the two poems, the major difference lies in the relationship between the speaker and the situation. Plath's speaker enacts the death in a ritualistic manner. Rich's speaker reflects upon death at a distance. Plath's poem is an "experience"; Rich's poem is "about experience" and does not measure up to her own criteria for poems. Whereas Rich's children are playacting death, Plath's speaker is more serious in her intent. Her desire to throw off her life becomes a longing for a return to the womb—the watery world of her recovery from the operation: "My body is a pebble to them, they tend it as water / Tends to the pebbles it must run over, smoothing them gently." Her belongings seem to "sink out of sight," while she feels as though she is drowning: "the water went over my head." Her "death" leads to a spiritual transformation: "I am a nun now, I have never been so pure." In the dramatic structure of Plath's poem, therefore, we enter the speaker's consciousness and know, by means of what she feels and perceives, the immediacy of the deathlike state.

Rich's attempts to achieve immediacy do not work as well. Employing direct address in her second stanza, she brings in as listeners the children of the first stanza:

> Nobody sleeps here, children.
> The little beds of white wrought iron
> and the tall, kind, faceless nurse

> are somewhere else, in a hospital
> or the dreams of prisoners of war

In the third stanza her speaker attempts to reenter the experience of childhood:

> In Pullmans of childhood we lay
> enthralled behind dark-green curtains
> and a little lamp burned blue
> all night for us.

Then she pulls away from this innocent mimicking of death-in-sleep to say in adult tones, "To stay here [the cemetery] forever is not like that." Rich's shifting point of view detracts from the effectiveness of the poem. Where Plath achieves a dramatic enactment of the theme, Rich is reduced to statement. "Not Like That" concludes: "The drawers of this trunk are empty. / They are all out of sleep up here." In phrasing, these lines are similar to Plath's "The tulips are too excitable, it is winter here." In Rich's poem, then, we detect echoes of Sylvia Plath's tone, phrasing, and approach to subject matter. In contrast to "Tulips," "Not Like That" does not succeed in making the situation believable.

While Adrienne Rich's interests may border Sylvia Plath's, her sensibility is quite different. For Plath, the death world she creates in "Tulips" was an essential part of the process of transformation. Jon Rosenblatt comments upon this process in his study of Plath: "In the initiatory imagination, the self must be violently purged, usually through the assumption of a fetal or infantile condition, before it can take on a new identity. Evidently, the strategy of ritual is to use the death impulses to generate a renewed desire to live."[8] Although Rich shares Plath's desire for transformation, she is not ultimately attracted by "death-impulses" as was Plath. When she takes Plath's approach to death as well as some of her phrasing, she ends up with a weak imitation. Plath's words and phrases appeal to Rich, mainly for their cleansing power in which "a subjective, personal rage blazes forth, never before seen in women's poetry. If it is unnerving it is also cathartic" (*ARP*, p. xii). Plath's vision, however, was too

intimately connected with a death wish; that is, she would risk
death for the desired rebirth. Rich's sensibility is not engaged by
her imaginative enactment of the death state. Instead, her vision
contemplates cleansing language itself. Concerned with ways
that language malfunctions, the poetic consciousness of Rich's
poems desires more vital communication. Rich returns to these
concerns in the last poem in the volume.

"Face to Face" (1965) imagines what is must have been like to
live in the relative isolation of the American wilderness:

> Never to be lonely like that—
> the Early American figure on the beach
> in black coat and knee-breeches
> scanning the didactic storm in privacy.

The opening conjecture—"Never to be lonely like that"—reveals a paradoxical yearning for a prior mode of existence. It is
not so much the geography that intrigues the speaker, but a way
of being in the world. Call it certitude: "one's claim / to be Law
and Prophets / for all that lawlessness. . . ." In this portrayal
"the Early American figure on the beach" seems slightly ridicu-
lous and the speaker's yearning, her sense of deprivation, meant
as irony. The irony crumbles in the last two stanzas:

> How people used to meet!
> starved, intense, the old
> Christmas gifts saved up till spring,
> and the old plain words,
>
> and each with his God-given secret,
> spelled out through months of snow and silence,
> burning under the bleached scalp; behind dry lips
> a loaded gun.

If people were so isolated from one another, the excitement of
coming together, of speaking, must have been extraordinary. For
this condition, then, the speaker can truly yearn. Language becomes almost too powerful, "a loaded gun" that could kill. The
last line suggests the perversions of repression and also calls to
mind the Emily Dickinson poem that begins "My Life—had

stood a Loaded Gun." Rich has referred elsewhere to this poem as "the real 'onlie begetter' of my thoughts . . . about Dickinson; a poem which I have mused over, repeated to myself, taken into myself over many years. I think it is a poem about possession by the daemon, about the dangers and risks of such possession if you are a woman, about the knowledge that power in a woman can seem destructive and that you cannot live without the daemon once it has possessed you. The archetype of the daemon as masculine is beginning to change, but it has been real for women up to now."[9] In this passage, Rich makes an implicit connection between Dickinson and herself. Dickinson's poem obsessed her because it deals with the subject of woman and power. Like Emily Dickinson, Rich for a long time regarded her poetic power as a destructive, masculine trait—a loaded gun. Thus the last stanza of "Face to Face" takes on the kind of echoes that are essential to Rich's concerns: language and power and the necessities of life. "A loaded gun" becomes, then, a clue to the relevance of the poem in the volume as a whole; that is, what it means to be both woman and poet.

In conclusion, Rich works through many issues involved with being a woman poet in *Necessities of Life*. In the beginning of the book she expresses her own ability to transform and the essential part that language has played in that transformation. She begins to take upon herself, in a conscious way, her destiny as a poet. This involves transforming her own silences—her unsaid words—as well as purifying the language. Further expression of the latter intent appears in her analysis of the cathartic effect of Sylvia Plath's and Diane Wakoski's poetry: "the blowtorch of language cleansing the rust and ticky-tacky and veneer from an entire consciousness" (*ARP*, p. xii). As a feminist poet, Adrienne Rich develops a similar force in her poetry, but *politicized*—a term she applies to Robin Morgan's *Monster* (1972)—and offered to other women engaged in the project of transformation of their lives. She meditates upon her position in many of the poems in *Necessities*, and she searches in others for positive, life-affirming uses of power ("I am in Danger—Sir—").

In some instances, she retains an identification of power with masculinity. But she will truly bring to fruition her power to transform when she can validate her creative power as naturally inherent in her womanhood, an issue she grapples with more openly in *Leaflets*.

CHAPTER 6

NO BETTER POETRY
IS WANTED:
LEAFLETS
(1969)

ADRIENNE RICH's *Leaflets* challenges our notions about the nature of poetry, both the forms it can (or should) assume and its "proper" content. American poetry, in particular, has not been overly receptive to political issues, and Rich's 1969 volume, for the most part, is determinedly political. In addition, she experiments quite radically with poetic form. Controversial in content and form, these poems also signify development in Rich's aesthetics of power. The three-part, chronological arrangement of the poems in *Leaflets* underscores that development. The opening poems were composed in 1965, followed by a few from 1966–67, but most were written in 1968. The sheer quantity of the 1968 poems attests to a renewed sense of poetic energy. Rich's productivity in 1968—her sense of her own poetic power—reflects a shift in her poetic consciousness from an allegiance to the male principle to an identification with the female principle as the locus of transforming power.

The opposite of the male principle, the female principle is traditionally defined as all that is dark and irrational in the human psyche. Closer to the animal or the instinctual, the female principle is most often considered inferior to the male principle or "higher" consciousness. Westerners especially have come to value the male principle of light or reason. In contrast, the female principle has been repressed or ignored becaue it is a reminder of our animal origins. In locating the female principle within herself, Adrienne Rich engages in a search that marks an important stage in her aesthetics of power. Her journey toward revaluing this contemned principle is the signal advance of *Leaflets*.

The shift from the male to the female principle can be charted from "Orion," which opens the volume, to "Abnegation," which closes the first section. In the second section, "Leaflets" both reinforces and advances the conclusions reached in "Abnegation" and prepares us for the experimental forms of part 3— "Ghazals: Homage to Ghalib."

Besides affirming the importance of the female principle in her aesthetic, Adrienne Rich also looks for and finds other women writers as models of poetic and personal behavior. "Charleston in the 1860's," for example, is derived from the diaries of Mary Boykin Chesnut. In this poem Rich confirms her own sense of desperate outrage at the political and social climate of the 1960s and concludes that there is "No imagination to forestall woe." *Leaflets* helps Rich rediscover the kind of imagination that can release her from a feeling of powerlessness. In addition to finding an American precursor, Rich looks abroad to the Yiddish poet Kadia Maldovsky in "There Are Such Springlike Nights" and to the Russian Anna Akhmatova in "Two Poems." Another Russian, Natalya Gorbanevskaya, appears in "For a Russian Poet." Rich's conscious search for female precursors and colleagues continues the quest begun in earlier volumes. What distinguishes these new additions is that she is looking for women poets who address political issues. Faced with the enormity of world problems, what can the poet do? Rich explores this question in her poems and concludes that, for her, poetic power makes sense only if her personal transformation through her art extends outward beyond the self. Rich comes to this understanding through a deeper awareness of her own womanhood and a poetic tradition for women, but especially through an affirmation of the female principle.

Rich's movement toward this principle comes from a long involvement with its opposite, as we discover in opening *Leaflets* to its first poem, "Orion" (1965). A winter constellation, Orion rises in the western sky. Huge and warriorlike, it provides an apt metaphor for Rich's insight that power is exhilarating. In contrast, the failures of ordinary human interaction are burdensome and debilitating. Powerfulness is, therefore, a desirable condition and may even block out the "bruise and blunder" of personal relationships. Adrienne Rich projects onto Orion her own sense of power, an awareness of the male principle within herself. Albert Gelpi's reading of "Orion" as an animus poem clarifies this awareness. Referring to Jungian theory, he says that "for a woman the animus represents her affinity with light as mind and spirit and her capacity for intellection and ego-consciousness" (*ARP*, p. 137). While Rich's female speaker admires the obvious excellence of Orion, she also recognizes his faults. His *machismo,* for example, emerges as comical. Even so, Orion's dynamic male energy attracts the speaker and she takes him in as she would a lover.

The beginning of the poem speaks of a long-term attraction:

> Far back when I went zig-zagging
> through tamarack pastures
> you were my genius, you
> my cast-iron Viking, my helmed
> lion-heart king in prison.

Over a span of time, minor tensions surface in the relationship between Rich's speaker and Orion, but they do not lead to disruption. This relationship has endured over time. While she may have idealized Orion as her "genius" in her youth, his brilliance no longer seems as perfect to her: "the stars in it are dim." Where once he was a "cast-iron Viking," now his great warrior pose appears silly and she calls his "sword / the last bravado you won't give over." Consciously, the speaker has matured in her perception of Orion. This consciousness is not powerful enough, however, to counter her visceral response: "as I throw back my head to take you in / an old transfusion happens again: / divine astronomy is nothing to it." Orion is Rich's muse: male, powerful, erotic, and energizing.

The center of the poem tells a different story. Orion's energy does not carry over to domestic life where Rich's speaker feels powerless in the extreme: "Indoors I bruise and blunder, / break faith, leave ill enough / alone, a dead child born in the dark." A failure in her human relationships, the speaker despairs at her impotence, that "dead child born in the dark." The larger world of Orion enters willy-nilly, destructive, and fragmentary: "frozen geodes / come showering down in the grate." The speaker's human dealings are sterile and nonproductive: "A man reaches behind my eyes / and finds them empty." The "transfusion" she receives from Orion does not revitalize her relationships with others or with herself, thus her self-loathing and anguish.

Life or art? This poem prefers art because of its control over emotion. Exhibiting exactly that control, the poem shifts from its chronicle of domestic despair back to Orion. He is a role model, an image of strength:

> Pity is not your forte.
> Calmly you ache up there
> pinned aloft in your crow's nest,
> my speechless pirate!
> You take it all for granted
> and when I look you back
>
> it's with a starlike eye
> shooting its cold and egotistical spear
> where it can do least damage.
> Breathe deep! No hurt, no pardon
> out here in the cold with you
> you with your back to the wall.

The speaker engages Orion as an equal, her "starlike eye / shooting its cold egotistical spear." In a womanly expression of concern, she adds, "where it can do least damage." Nonetheless, this ending disappoints because it fails to address the polarities

93

of the poem. In other words, Rich engages a dialectic but does not move toward a synthesis. The two conditions in the poem are perceived as irreconcilable. When she chooses one, she transcends the earthly condition of "bruise and blunder" and ends up in the heavens with Orion. His back may be "to the wall," but he is splendid. So, we might add, is Rich's handling of her poetic materials.

As an artistic expression of a mind in conflict, the poem is, quite clearly, superb. Synthesis is not that easy to come by and Rich's extended metaphor of Orion is striking enough to invest the poem with its essential unity. If the "frozen geodes / . . . showering down in the grate" do not convince us imagistically (are we to believe that Orion sent them spinning?), nonetheless they convey a sense of the world falling apart outdoors as well as in. There is precious little Rich's speaker can do about this fragmentation. She is a woman, after all, and powerless.

Should we even identify the speaker as female? Textual evidence is slim. Beside the inherent eroticism of her acceptance of Orion's "transfusion," there is her fear of hurting others. Might not a male be similarly concerned? A recent essay by Alicia Ostriker helps us to understand Rich's persona and her conflict as typically female. Women poets, Ostriker says (she cites Diane Wakoski), often render their poet personas as male, "a proud, controlling, even predatory force," while the "woman" in their poems is seen as "pathetically needy." Ostriker goes on to clarify the nature of this polarity in Wakoski's poetry: "The two sides of herself are appropriately also an all and a nothing, a strong and a weak." Ostriker calls this "the All or Nothing syndrome in female romantic fantasies."[1]

Clearly, Rich participates in this syndrome. You can be an artist ("cold egotistical"), or you can direct your energies toward being a loving human being. Later, she will call these "false" alternatives and say that love itself is in need of "re-vision" (ARP, p. 97). "Orion," as written in 1965, is a moving display of the experience of woman as creative artist and the subsequent exhilaration and despair she feels. It suggests that along with revisioning "love," Adrienne Rich also needs to call into question her identification, as an artist, with the male principle, a perception shaped by her reading of Gottfried Benn's essay "Artists and Old Age," as she notes in a later gloss on "Orion."

Benn advises the modern artist: "Don't lose sight of the cold and egotistical element in your mission. . . . With your back to the wall, careworn and weary, in the gray light of the void, read Job and Jeremiah and keep going" (*ARP*, p. 36). Rich adopts Benn's phrasing for her last stanza, and while the "true grit" pose seems as existentially Romantic as the "cast-iron Viking" of stanza 1, she ends the poem before she can debunk it.

It will take her three years and the writing of "Abnegation" before Rich can begin to free herself from the hold of "Orion." "Abnegation" (1968) is Rich at her intellectual best, saying that her intellectuality is a burden she could do without. Like "Orion," the poem operates as a dialectic, yet this time synthesis is achieved. The key image in the poem is a red fox, a vixen seen "dancing in the half-light among the junipers." The speaker responds to the vixen's femaleness and instinctual behavior first by contrasting herself with the fox, then by identifying with her. The fox represents the female principle. When Rich's speaker considers the charms of the vixen, she cannot help relaxing her allegiance to her own heritage—a "westernness" that has led to self-abnegation.

> The red fox, the vixen
> dancing in the half-light among the junipers,
> wise-looking in a sexy way,
> Egyptian-supple in her sharpness—
> what does she want
> with the dreams of dead vixens,
> the apotheosis of Reynard,
> the literature of fox-hunting?
> Only in her nerves the past
> sings, a thrill of self-preservation.
> I go along down the road
> to a house nailed together by Scottish
> Covenanters, instinct mortified

in a virgin forest,
and she springs toward her den
every hair on her pelt alive
with tidings of the immaculate present.
They left me a westernness,
a birthright, a redstained, ravelled
afghan of sky.
She has no archives,
no heirlooms, no future
except death
and I could be more
her sister than theirs
who chopped their way across these hills
—a chosen people.

Rich's speaker is drawn to the vixen because she seems free. She also appears to be having a good time: she *dances*. There is a vital force in the vixen that comes across as intelligent and earthy at the same time. "Wise-looking in a sexy way," although marred by the language of display ads, captures the dichotomies nicely embodied in the one creature. As if to correct her jingle-like diction, Rich adds, "Egyptian-supple in her sharpness," a wonderful line that brings to mind ancient animal carvings and belly dancers at the same time. *Sharpness* balances *supple,* neither term outweighing the other. Seemingly, the fox has it all: a harmonious balancing of opposing forces.

The speaker's questions poke gentle fun at her own obsessions with the past, obsessions that point out the burden of consciousness: that which remembers, projects, compares, and stores up in a quantifiable way. How absurd for the vixen to refer to "the literature of fox-hunting"—that is, to live her life in a manner distanced from direct experience. How typical for a poet like Adrienne Rich to have a consciousness where such materials would be filed and stored. In contrast she sets the vixen: "Only in her nerves the past / sings, a thrill of self-preservation."

The placement of "only" at the beginning of an apparently assertive statement creates multiple ambiguities and the reader has to negotiate their claims for importance. It could read: "Only in *her* nerves the past / sings . . . ," which would focus attention on the femaleness of the fox. This reading concentrates our awareness on Rich's shift from an overemphasis on maleness as vitality to her new understanding of the value of female energy. Or it could read: "Only in her *nerves* the past / sings . . . ," which would highlight the nonrational element. Consciousness thus becomes a component of body awareness and the mind/ body split disappears. Another reading might be: "Only in her nerves the *past* / sings . . . ," which would locate the meaning of the sentence in its lineation. Where is the past? Only in her nerves, not in books, dreams, or fantasy ("the apotheosis of Reynard"). The line raises the ante of the poem from a light-hearted description of a fox to a poetic exploration of the meaning of the past. The weight of the line pushes us to this reading because *only* drives toward the line-breaking *past*. Syntactically, however, the line moves through its enjambment and we have a final alternative: "Only in her nerves the past / *sings* . . ." This is the most aesthetically satisfying emphasis because it highlights the joy of the vixen's existence, complements the "dancing" of line 2 and establishes a rationale for the speaker's awakening to the desirability of freeing herself into a condition of vital connection with the past. If the past *sings,* it is not a dreary burden, but a creative expression. The tensions in the poem reinforce this final reading.

In contrast to the vixen, the speaker describes herself as a plodding, dull creature. No dancing and singing for her: "I go along down the road." The drabness of Rich's verb shifts the tone as the speaker reflects seriously on what she has become because of her Protestant heritage. Rich's "Scottish Covenanters" could be any of our Puritan forbears. This is a poem by an American, after all, and while the perception of the Puritans is stereotypical, it is true to the cultural pattern most Americans feel. The phrase, "instinct mortified," also underscores the significance of the vixen, who stands for the opposite. When the next three lines return to the image of the vixen, Rich captures the animal's vibrancy and immediacy: "she springs toward her den / every hair on her pelt alive / with tidings of the immaculate

97

present." The odd word choice of *immaculate* is stimulated, perhaps, by the reference to the "virgin forest" in the previous quatrain. Whereas *virgin* is common parlance for a forest that has never been cut into, *immaculate* is hardly an ordinary term for the "present" of this poem—1968, the year of the assassinations of Martin Luther King and Robert Kennedy. We have to grant the poem its imaginative truth that the present moment—in the making—is immaculate, for it has not been written upon, thus unstained. In its advocacy for seizing the moment and its Zenlike perceptions of time, this poem is very much of its period.

When lines 18–20 cite the speaker's heritage, we are not surprised at the denigration of "westernness, / a birthright, a red-stained, ravelled / afghan of sky." The previous image now comes clearer as the result of the explicit contrast. If there is any "birthright" that westerners hold in common it is the Judeo-Christian heritage with its emphasis on sin, a concept so pervasive that the sky itself appears tainted by the fall of man.

The poem advances through its polarities, and when the focus shifts back to the vixen, emphasis falls upon what she lacks: "no archives, / no heirlooms, no future, / except death." But for the shock of the last phrase, we can appreciate these "lacks" as advantages. The speaker clearly wishes to be similarly relieved of her burdensome sense of history and the religious, cultural, and social heritage of western civilization. We are drawn up short at the "no future / except death," not wanting the lively, sexy vixen to remind us of the grim reaper. The reminder, nonetheless, undercuts any possibility of romanticizing the animal and the instinctual. The "thrill of self-preservation" is a thrill, after all, only in the context of potential hazard.

Knowing all this and more, thrusting behind herself any possibilities of transcendence or salvation in the *old* way, the speaker approaches self-recognition at the end of the poem. The pole that attracts, its appeal magnetic, is the vixen's. "I could be more / her sister than theirs," shifts the speaker's allegiance. Rich would have us understand this allegiance both on a personal scale (it is her self-transformation from Orionhood that is the subject of the poem) and in a larger, political context. The "Scottish Covenanters"—those westerners "who chopped their way across these hills / —a chosen people"—are no kin of hers. Rich rejects a cultural and religious heritage that regards the wilderness as something to be tamed or chartered and forbears who felt divinely ordained to do so.

"Abnegation" must be understood, ultimately, as a political poem that originates from a deeply felt personal perception. The poetic consciousness of Adrienne Rich moves naturally toward themes of the broadest possible scope. We must remember, as well, that this poem was written in 1968—when social and political issues rose to the forefront of the nation's consciousness in civil rights demonstrations and in ongoing protests against the war in Vietnam. Environmental concerns were soon to follow. Where had this nation of so much promise gone so wrong?

Rich locates one possible answer in America's being cut off from everything the vixen represents in her poem. She is femaleness in a world dominated by a masculinity grown grotesque. Power-as-force can no longer govern if the world is to survive. The vixen is also that part of the human psyche which we name the unconscious or instinctual. Closer to the primal roots of existence, the vixen is compellingly alive. The speaker discovers through the vixen her own existentialism; being is becoming and death the only certainty. The image of the vixen also speaks for the liberation of a vibrant sexuality. The "Scottish Covenanters" with their propensities for cutting and nailing are distinctly unattractive, the inhibitions imposed by their fear of sensuality something to be thrown off. Rich throws off inhibitions in other ways as well, as further examination of *Leaflets* will attest.

Leaflets charts the evolution of Rich's personal, aesthetic, and political values from 1965 to 1968. This development can be most clearly seen in the two poems "Orion" and "Abnegation," the dynamic relationship between them containing the essence of the book as a whole. The most significant tendency is toward the female principle. By 1968, Rich has achieved a different understanding of femaleness and power, maleness and power. After she writes "Abnegation," she can no longer write in the old forms; she is compelled to find new ones.

Her title poem is paradigmatic of those necessary changes. In the five sections of "Leaflets," each part takes a different approach, especially in lineation. In section 1 there is no recognizable narrative, only an attempt to capture the fluctuations of a mind—Adrienne Rich's mind—confronted by the stark impassivity of the universe. Out of that confrontation comes a reaffirmation of personal and artistic goals:

> The big star, and that other
> lonely on black glass
> overgrown with frozen
> lesions, endless night
> the Coal Sack gaping
> black veins of ice on the pane
> spelling a word:
>   Insomnia
> not manic but ordinary
> to start out of sleep
> turning off and on
> this seasick neon
> vision, this
> division
>
> the head clears of sweet smoke
> and poison gas
>
> life without caution
> the only worth living
> love for a man
> love for a woman
> love for the facts
> protectless
>
> that self-defense be not
> the arm's first motion
>
> memory not only
> cards of identity

that I can live half a year
as I have never lived up to this time—
Chekhov coughing up blood almost daily
the steamer edging in toward the penal colony
chained men dozing on deck
five forest fires lighting the island

lifelong that glare, waiting.

Initially, "Leaflets" appears formless. Stanzas have been abandoned for clusters of lines. Sentences are fragmented, if there are sentences at all. Punctuation appears, disappears. The disorder of this apparently formless form is its artistic order. Reading "Leaflets" gives about as much pleasure—if that is what we are after—as being confronted, for the first time, by a Jackson Pollock painting. We expect the poet to do more work for her readers and to create an ordered sensibility. Rich refuses. This refusal is her newborn power.

Even so, the opening of part 1 of "Leaflets" is typical Rich, particularly for readers of "Orion." Looking out at the night sky and locating stars is one of Rich's obsessions, for the poet always maintains a sense of a larger whole on which to frame her personal concerns. This night she is drawn to a dark nebula called "the Coal Sack" that appears as a hole in the Milky Way. For bleakness, this opening cluster has found an appropriate image. When the poem telescopes backward to a closer view of "black veins of ice on the pane / spelling a word: / Insomnia," we are nonplussed. Is *this* what the poem is about? Someone is driven awake in the middle of the night by a nightmare of loneliness so vast the stellar universe encompasses it. This reading seems appropriate because *Leaflets* presents other insomniacs in "Night in the Kitchen," "5:30 A.M.," and "The Break."

In contrast to these other poems, insomnia in "Leaflets" signifies disturbance "not manic but ordinary." Rich's speaker is at pains not to enter the poem in the first-person singular. The "I" is refused by numerous syntactic dodges and the choice of *ordinary* to stress the commonality of disturbance. Something is happening out there and it feels bad: a "seasick neon / vision, / this division." She will not tell us what this division is; we have to take the slight clues offered, particularly her reference to the stars. "The big star" could be the North Star, the navigator's guide. If it is "overgrown with frozen lesions," it can no longer give clear direction. Clarity must be found elsewhere. If the Coal Sack *gapes*, it is ugly and frightening. The loneliness of the poem is cosmic; the division, a sense of being separated from that which used to give sustenance. There is no Emersonian sense of oneness with Nature here. No solitary Thoreau finding at Walden a "sweet and beneficent society in Nature." The insomniac disturbance of this poem can be located in a "sea-sick . . . vision" positing an absolute alienation.

While "Leaflets" may begin with this profound sickness of the soul, it does not remain bleak. Somehow, out of this disturbance comes clarity: "the head clears of sweet smoke and poison gas." With no narrative line to hang these images on except for the insomniac gazing at stars, we must accept their pure suggestiveness. They imply a political context with the "poison gas" of street demonstrations and also with the social phenomenon of "turning on" in the sixties. This turning on was also a tuning out and the poem rejects that position. The subsequent lines are thrilling in their declaration of "life without caution / the only worth living," and we are reminded of the vixen speeding toward her den, "every hair on her pelt alive."

The fulcrum of the poem—that point upon which it turns toward an affirmation—comes in the simple but stunning statement "that self-defense be not / the arm's first motion." These lines appear to come out of nowhere and we are not prepared to be found out in such a penetrating fashion. Of course, the power of these lines comes from the poet's self-recognition. That self insists upon "memory not only / cards of identity." The Who-I-Am can be known only in relationship to the past and to others; this poem, therefore, advances beyond the position of "Abnegation." Significantly, the poet turns to another writer to help her formulate that new sense of being in the world. Chekhov is her role model. Clearly she admires him for journeying to Sakhalin, "the penal colony" mentioned at the close of the section. He is a challenge, someone to measure oneself against. The "forest fires" he sees "lighting the island" portray that challenge, and Rich ends this section with a reference to the light they emanate. They are beacons: "lifelong that glare, waiting." Both threatening and attractive, Rich's concluding image suggests a greater openness to experience than offered by the image cluster in the opening of the poem: stars that signified nothing, led to nothing. "Leaflets" portrays the mind of the poet in the process of a change from negation to affirmation. Rich's forms demand a higher degree of involvement than ever before from her readers, who therefore become a part of the poem's making. Complex and fascinating, the poet will not be lonely, but draws us along with her.

A brief look at the final section of the poem indicates where Rich takes this opening charge to live a more deeply engaged and "uncautious" life. Questions come to mind: Does her affirmation hold? What is the significance of the "Leaflets" of the title? What do the Chekhovian beacons summon her toward?

Section 5 of "Leaflets" is about the value of poetry and was written during the winter and spring of 1968, explosive months in the life of the poet. A speaker appears in the form of a first-person singular, an "I" so close to the "I" of the poet that it seems false to continue to pretend there is a persona or mask here. The poet-speaker then addresses a "you" who told her once "that poetry is nothing sacred / —no more sacred that is / than other things in your life." Once the argument is opened, the poet accepts the challenge and answers, "Yes, if life is uncorrupted / no better poetry is wanted." If life is sacred, so too poetry. If life is not sacred, but corrupt, poetry is needed to pull it out of the morass. The value of poetry inheres in its ability to uplift and enlighten. With that understood, the poem moves to its climax, which reads like a manifesto:

> I want this to be yours
> in the sense that if you find and read it
> it will be there in you already
> and the leaflet then merely something

    to leave behind, a little leaf
in the drawer of a sublet room.
    What else does it come down to
but handing on scraps of paper
    little figurines or phials
no stronger than the dry clay they are baked in
    yet more than dry clay or paper
because the imagination crouches in them.
    If we needed fire to remind us
that all true images
    were scooped out of the mud
where our bodies curse and flounder
    then perhaps that fire is coming
to sponge away the scribes and time-servers
    and much that you would have loved will be lost as well
before you could handle it and know it
    just as we almost miss each other
in the ill cloud of mistrust, who might have touched
    hands quickly, shared food or given blood
for each other. I am thinking how we can use what we have
    to invent what we need.

The lines of section 5 dart in and out, challenging our sense of form while creating their own form. There are no rules, these lines say. Poetry is not sacred: it does not need to rhyme; it can sound like prose. But we must not be taken in by the casual manner, the direct speech. Something deeply serious is going on here and poetic forms are the least of it. Rich's manifesto asserts a radical classicism that Homer could embrace.

    The impulse of the poem is straightforward: "I want this to be yours." *This* is the poem, something one finds and reads. No big deal. Reading the poem should awaken something in the reader that is "already . . . there." No need then to keep its external form. The poem as "leaflet" can be left behind. Rich's stance might shock some and it is meant to do so. If poems are "scraps of paper," then they certainly are not sacred, and we find the poet has now become the poetic scoffer she introduced earlier. She tricks us into agreeing that poetry is, indeed, profane. So, too, are other art forms: "little figurines or phials." Once she has reached this point, her images propel the poem into meta-physical regions. Indeed, "the imagination crouches" in all art forms. *Crouches* reminds us of the power of the imagination to leap.

If, as Robert Frost stated, poetry operates by "feats of association," then lines 13–25 give us graphic display of the poetic imagination in action. Nonlinear, dynamic, and lightning-fast, this section calls to mind, once again, the nature of the vixen and the female principle. To analyze it, we must deliberately slow down and note the syntax: the long first sentence that builds by accretions like the rings on a tree growing outward to encompass larger and larger dimensions. The first *if* clause allows entrance to imaginative supposition, and we find ourselves agreeing that, *yes,* "all true images / were scooped out of the mud." Rich's aesthetic is radical in that she goes to the root or primal source of art. Just so, she reminds us that we come from the selfsame mud "where our bodies curse and flounder." Might not our destiny be the same as that of the "true images"? If so, we must endure a similar firing process. Thus artistic transformation is connected to personal transformation, not just for the poet but for the rest of us who read her "leaflets." In the process of this firing, destruction occurs: "much that you would have loved will be lost as well." With this gesture, the syntax accretes a new ring of meaning and Rich returns to the important love theme of section 1.

Here, however, the lines assume a negative tone: "we almost *miss* each other," "*ill* cloud of *mistrust,*" and "*might* have touched." Despite its negativity, this poem is invested with a tremendous desire for a loving community. The alienation of section 1 must be transcended and the poet, operating to her fullest capacity (like Chekhov), imagines her public role as reminding us of those "higher" possibilities. No matter how gross or profane the materials at hand, there is no cause for alarm: "all true images / were scooped out of the mud." Thus the last sentence of the poem takes on its impact: "I am thinking how we can use what we have / to invent what we need." All that we have is each other. No longer the solitary insomniac filled with angst in a frightening universe, the poet is charged with a renewed sense of her poetic function. That role is public, even messianic. The "I" melds into a "we." Adrienne Rich's poetic persona is not Emersonian but Whitmanesque. The vistas she imagines are democratic and her ethos a personal and public transformation.

As the most substantive exploration of Rich's current aesthetic position, "Leaflets" fittingly gives its title to the volume as a whole and pulls the remaining poems into clearer focus. The disturbing yet productive year of 1968 also saw Rich's first use of the ghazal as a poetic form. Comprising the third and final section of the volume, the "Ghazals: Homage to Ghalib" are based upon the female principle as the locus of transforming power and contribute to Rich's developing aesthetic.

In her preface to the ghazal section, Rich explains the literary influence of Ghalib and defines her own method:

> This poem began to be written after I read Aijaz Ahmad's literal English versions of the work of the Urdu poet Mirza Ghalib, 1797–1869. While the structure and metrics used by Ghalib are much stricter than mine, I have adhered to his use of a minimum five couplets to a ghazal, each couplet being autonomous and independent of the others. The continuity and unity flow from the associations and images playing back and forth among the couplets in any single ghazal.

Her use of the passive voice in the first sentence suggests something about the nature of the ghazal as poetic form. Composed in an intense period between July 12 and August 8, 1968, these poems were something that "began to be written." Thus she stresses the lack of conscious choice. Presented as spontaneous jottings, though far from it, the ghazals reinforce Rich's present aesthetic of the "leaflet" nature of poems. Even so, she adheres to a form and finds validation for the kind of method she experimented with in "Leaflets." In the ghazals, "continuity and unity flow from the associations and images." Employing this associational method, Rich forges a stronger link with that part of the female principle which is nonlogical, nonlinear and nonprescriptive. While Rich does even more with the ghazal form in

The Will to Change, a look at a typical ghazal will indicate how the form creates a new kind of poetic energy for the poet.

In the ghazal dated 7/24/68:i, Rich deals with the subject of nature through a variety of images, from trees and flowers to human sexuality. Her theme is separation from nature and the consequent sense of alienation and powerlessness. Each couplet, as in the traditional English form, is a complete idea within itself. Although its couplets are separated from one another on the page, the ghazal's flow of associations creates a unity of desire to discover deeper, fuller ways of connecting with one's self, with others, and with larger wholes:

> The sapling springs, the milkweed blooms: obsolete Nature.
> In the woods I have a vision of asphalt, blindly lingering.
>
> I hardly know the names of the weeds I love.
> I have forgotten the names of so many flowers.
>
> I can't live at the hems of that tradition—
> will I last to try the beginning of the next?
>
> Killing is different now: no fingers round the throat.
> No one feels the wetness of the blood on his hands.
>
> When we fuck, there too are we remoter
> than the fucking bodies of lovers used to be?
>
> How many men have touched me with their eyes
> more hotly than they later touched me with their lips.

The associations can be tracked fairly easily from couplet to couplet by means of the imagery. The "sapling" and the "milkweed" initiate a type of natural image that the "weeds" and "flowers" of the second couplet carry on. In both, as well, the speaker experiences the same alienation from the natural world; she thinks of asphalt in the woods and has "forgotten the names of so many flowers." The third couplet cuts into the poignancy of these feelings, abandons image for statement, and places the first two couplets into the context of "tradition." At a point of transition, the speaker expresses doubt about "that tradition," most likely a belief in the natural world as a source of rejuvenation. In other words, the Romantic and Transcendentalist tradition of English and American idealism no longer works for Adrienne Rich.

She feels "at the hems of that tradition" and nothing viable has yet taken its place. The next three couplets concern what is lacking. All the images deal with a separation from nature—in this part of the poem, human nature. Even the killer feels no "blood on his hands." The actual kiss is less passionate than the imagined; it is like being in the woods and thinking of asphalt.

In this ghazal, and in Rich's general use of the form, the poet creates a richness of association because she works with "independent, autonomous" couplets. By itself, each couplet conveys a clear idea or feeling. In the sequence, the meaning of each flows into the next with an alteration provided by a new image, a contrary idea, or a parallel idea. Thus a cumulative enlargement occurs. The form achieves its effects because of its insistence upon placing separate things together. The ghazal says that these separations exist and at the same time that everything connects. The form, therefore, makes possible "feats of association," creating for the poet a new kind of energy. In her next book, she continues using the ghazal form, attesting to its significance for her at this time.

Rich's use of the ghazal form underscores the theme of power as it is handled in *Leaflets*. We understand the poet's need for new sources of power in the particular context of the social and political upheaval of the sixties. At home were the clashes of the civil rights movement, abroad the specter of the Vietnam War: the senseless destruction, the incalculable human waste, the degradation of being part of a superpower so morally turgid. On the more personal level, there are also strong suggestions of marital discord. What else could the poet feel but her "back against the wall."

Rich has not developed a feminist consciousness yet and thus identifies her stance with the male principle—Orion. Toughness gets her through. As the volume progresses, however, there are signs of regret over something lost because of the rigidity of her stance. The vixen is an archetypal image of the loss of an instinctual, female self with whom Rich would like to establish contact.

Poems such as "Leaflets" and the ghazals move closer to a more instinctual, spontaneous form. The vixen has, to a certain extent, returned from her exile. That is, Adrienne Rich recognizes her abnegation of the "shadow" anima and adopts the ghazal form. Even in the ghazals, however, there are signs that she has not found what Robert Bly deems the "special channels" of the senses which will allow the shadow's return: "So many minds in search of bodies / groping their way among artificial limbs." It is only in the last ghazal, written to A.H.C., her husband Alfred Conrad, that Rich opens up her language to sensual delight and to human imperfection. The last two couplets are particularly significant. In the following, she embraces the "bruise and blunder" of the human condition: "How frail we are, and yet, dispersed, always returning, / the barnacles they keep scraping from the warship's hull." The metaphor of humans as barnacles—not just on any ship but on a "warship's hull"—pulls together several strands in the volume. Small, yet tenacious, those barnacle energies pit their obstinacy against the forces of destruction. In this couplet Rich focuses on that persistence and not on the failure to defeat the war machine.

In the last ghazal, the senses dominate: "The hairs on your breast curl so lightly as you lie there, / while the strong heart goes on pounding in its sleep." The imagery of this couplet leads her to the instinctual, which is, of course, the deeper sensuality. The sound of the heart combines with the sight and the feel of the man's chest hair. To deepen the sensuous quality of the imagery, music plays a key role. The alliteration of *lightly* and *lie* joins with *curl* to shape the melody. In *breast* and in *pounding* and *sleep*, the poet achieves the deeper beat she wants through the harder consonantal sounds. And, in contrast to "Leaflets," where the insomniac feels a terminal isolation, the sounds of the beating heart have an attentive listener.

Ending *Leaflets* with this particular couplet, Adrienne Rich signifies that she will keep open the channels of her senses so that the shadow energies can enter her poetry. Her personal and poetic power will expand to the extent that she allows the vixen to enter her consciousness. In this volume, therefore, Rich begins to sense how profoundly the female principle shapes her definition of womanly power and the aesthetics of her poetry.

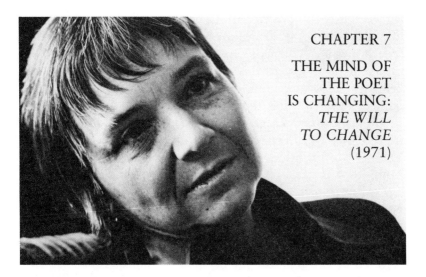

CHAPTER 7

THE MIND OF
THE POET
IS CHANGING:
*THE WILL
TO CHANGE*
(1971)

ADRIENNE RICH titles her sixth book of poetry *The Will to Change*, announcing both her purpose and the influence of Charles Olson, who writes in "The Kingfishers," "What does not change / is the will to change." Primarily, Rich wants to change herself. Because she is a poet, the changes she effects in herself reveal themselves in her poetry and, ultimately (this is the poet's wish), affect her audience as well. To achieve the changes she desires, Rich feels she must integrate more fully the woman she is with the poet she has become, a project she has been engaged upon both consciously and unconsciously since her first book of poems in 1951. In the words of "Planetarium," Rich achieves this integration when she experiences herself as "an instrument in the shape of a woman / trying to translate pulsations into images / for the relief of the body / and the reconstruction of the mind." Ezra Pound called poets the "antennae of the race"; in Rich's metaphor she becomes something similar— a transmitter of bodily "relief" and mental transformation. Her major literary influence, however, is Charles Olson and the theory of projective verse he articulated in the 1950s.

Metaphorically, the term *projective* implies a driving forward or outward—not an *im*-plosion but an *ex*-plosion. In order to achieve Olsonian projectivity in language, the poet must abandon the abstractions of "logos, or discourse" and come closer to speech rhythms. Olson prefers "language as the act of the instant" rather than "language as the act of thought about the instant" because the former is more like speech, thus more lively and immediate.[1] He states that the poem which adheres to speech rhythms must be "a high energy construct and, at all points, an energy discharge" (*The Poetics of the New American Poetry*, p. 148). Olson means, to put it simply, spontaneity and freedom from propriety and restraint. His definition of poetry coincides with Wordsworth's "spontaneous overflow of powerful feelings" but not with the adjoining "recollected in tranquility." Olson wants mind and feeling in poetry but not considered thought, an obvious reaction against the late refinement of T. S. Eliot in such poems as "The Four Quartets." Olson's theory of projective verse may be seen as a rejection of Eliotic elegance and the highly intellectual, poetic discourse that dominated the literary consciousness of the midtwentieth century, including much of Rich's early poetry.

Like Olson, Adrienne Rich recoiled from the overemphasis upon intellect in poetry, including her own work. For her, this emphasis meant an adherence to the male principle as the source of light or consciousness. Turning toward the female principle—the nonrational or instinctual in the human psyche—and finding it a source of power, Rich increased her receptivity to projective verse. Together these influences led her to make certain assumptions about change and about the poet's power. "Change" in *The Will to Change* (1969) means transformation, not merely "something different" but an actual restructuring of the mind—her mind, and subsequently, other minds. As a poet, Rich has the power to affect other minds; she knows this and accepts it as a poetic "right." Thus she says in "The Blue Ghazals," "If I thought of my words as changing minds, hadn't my mind also to suffer changes?" Projective verse provides the poetic vehicle for these changes, Olson's theory being the impulse behind the various poetic strategies adopted in this volume. David Kalstone notes that this "book struggles to find forms—among the short poems of the first part, letters, 'images,' a 'photograph,' pieces, and finally . . . a 'Shooting Script.' "[2] All these are open rather than closed forms, characterized by spontaneity instead of planned, rational discourse.

In addition to its technical experiments to "restructure the mind," *The Will to Change* marks Rich as a political poet, both in her choice of subject matter and in larger thematic issues. *Leaflets,* her preceding volume, contained signs of the same direction. In both volumes, Rich is overt about her politics, an urban radicalism that grew out of her involvement in civil rights and antiwar demonstrations and in teaching in the SEEK (open admission) Program at City College, New York, in the late sixties. About this last activity, she wrote a penetrating essay in 1972 that assesses the potential effects of language study upon those not ordinarily allowed access to higher education. The following passage from that essay also underlines some of the key themes in *The Will to Change:*

> At the bedrock of my thinking about [open admissions] is the sense that language is power, and that, as Simone Weil says, those who suffer from injustice most are the least able to articulate their suffering; and that the silent majority, if released into language, would not be content with a perpetuation of the conditions which have betrayed them. But this notion hangs on a special conception of what it means to be released into language: not simply learning the jargon of an elite, fitting unexceptionably into the status quo, but learning that language can be used as a means of changing reality. (*On Lies, Secrets, and Silence,* p. 67)

For the poet, "language is power." Could not the same be true for the ghetto child? If language is the quintessential human activity, then exercise of language is what makes us more fully human: the shapers of our lives rather than the victims of forces beyond our control. Rich's poetic sensibility extends quite naturally into the political sphere in her espousal of personal liberty and freedom from oppression. Politically and personally, "the jargon of an elite" is inimical to transformation. If this belief is at the "bedrock level of [her] thinking" about her students, it follows that Adrienne Rich would avoid the language of "an elite" in her own poetry and be open to experimental forms.

Charles Olson's advocacy of poems as "high-energy constructs" would, therefore, appeal to Adrienne Rich. She had already recognized in herself a "westernness" that had come to mean restriction and denial of regenerative life-forces. *The Will to Change* is close to *Leaflets* in this respect. If anything, the nonlinear associative techniques that were the sign of the female principle in the earlier volume are developed more fully in these later poems. Because Rich connects such techniques with femaleness and with transformation we can also regard this volume as a development of a particular aspect of her aesthetics of power.

In *Leaflets*, Rich came to regard womanliness as a positive factor and a source of creative power. *The Will to Change* advances these themes she had been moving toward since her first books of poetry. In her first volume, she had to adopt the covertness of the woman writer's double-voiced discourse and in her second, the quiet subversion of her male literary progenitors. At the same time, she was consciously searching for a female poetic tradition. As she became a mature poet, these strategies no longer appeared necessary. Nor does she focus upon woman's silence as a compelling issue. By 1969, the first flowering of the women's movement had made this issue moot. Women were not as silent anymore; some were even radical activists. Transformations had occurred and women had experienced them. To some, of course, this womanly activity was threatening—even monstrous. Rich addresses this issue in the centerpiece of the present volume, "Planetarium." In the same poem, Rich presents a female role model, Caroline Herschel, the astronomer. Rich's meditations upon Herschel lead her to deeper insights about women and about her own role as a woman poet.

"Planetarium" is an ambitious poem and Rich's most overtly feminist to date. Written in the watershed year of 1968, as were many of the *Leaflets* poems, it treats the subject of women as "monsters," and while Rich regards it as a companion piece to

"Orion" (*ARP*, p. 97), it also extends the themes of "Snapshots of a Daughter-in-Law." Instead of bewailing the fact that "she's long about her coming," Rich discovers a marvelous role model in Caroline Herschel (1750–1848), who "in her 98 years" was "to discover 8 comets." By entering directly into metaphor, adopting speech rhythms, and freeing herself almost entirely from standard punctuation, Rich develops the form of the poem as projective verse. Note the first twenty-five lines:

> A woman in the shape of a monster
> A monster in the shape of a woman
> the skies are full of them
>
> a woman   'in the snow
> among the Clocks and instruments
> or measuring the ground with poles'
>
> in her 98 years to discover
> 8 comets
>
> she whom the moon ruled
> like us
> levitating into the night sky
> riding the polished lenses
>
> Galaxies of women, there
> doing penance for impetuousness
> ribs chilled
> in those spaces   of the mind
>
> An eye,
>   'virile, precise and absolutely certain'
>   from the mad webs of Uranusborg
>   encountering the NOVA
>
> every impulse of light exploding
> from the core
> as life flies out of us
>
>   Tycho whispering at last
>   'Let me not seem to have lived in vain.'

Central to the poem is the image of "woman in the shape of a monster"—even Caroline Herschel, "she whom the moon ruled / like us." Subsequently, Rich develops a witch metaphor and adopts its action verbs: instead of riding a broom, Herschel is "riding the polished lenses." Because she does not stop the poem to spell out the connection for us, the poem enters directly into metaphor. In a gloss on projective verse and its adherents, Hugh Kenner points out that poets in the Pound era "perceived that the poetic energy, something new on the poet's page, was discernible in the unstated connections between phrases."[3] In "Planetarium" unstated connections inhere in Rich's handling of the witch metaphor.

By intimating that Herschel, the discoverer of eight comets, was a witch, Rich transforms the concept. The witch metaphor is important to Rich as a woman poet because through it she removes the onus from all those women who have been "labelled harpy, shrew and whore" ("Snapshots"), validating their "aberrant" (because female) energies through a process of revision. Rich defines this process as "the act of looking back, of seeing with fresh eyes" and describes re-vision as "an act of survival. Until we can understand the assumptions in which we are drenched we cannot know ourselves. And this drive to self-knowledge, for woman, is more than a search for identity: it is part of her refusal of the self-destructiveness of male-dominated society" (*ARP*, p. 90). To see Caroline Herschel as a witch, therefore, and by implication to view positively the "monstrous" energies of women, Adrienne Rich comes closer to validating her equally aberrant desire to speak as a poet—even though she is female. *The Will to Change* marks an openness not only in Rich's style, but in what she is willing to imagine for herself and other women. Thus content breaks with traditional modes of thought and behavior. Her liberties with syntax and diction mirror a similar direction in her style.

In "Planetarium" Rich's handling of tenses is as dextrous as her use of metaphor. Nowhere does time interfere with what Olson calls the "immediate, contemporary . . . acting-on-you of the poem." The poem begins in the present: "the skies *are* full of" women/monsters, or witches. Lines 4–6 shift to Caroline Herschel, 1750–1848, yet the tense is contemporaneous with the opening and indicated by the present participle "measuring."

Likewise lines 9–12 employ present participles in "levitating" and "riding." The poet uses the present tense here—even with a past event—to indicate that Herschel occupies her mind at the same time as the women in the shape of monsters. She returns to these women in lines 13–16, continuing the witch/monster metaphor and the presentness of the "galaxies of women, there" *now.* Lines 17–20 move back to Herschel but as if she were in the present, via the present participle, "*encountering* the NOVA." In lines 21–23, time is telescoped: the past and the present linked in "light exploding" from the nova encountered by Herschel and in life "as it *flies* out of us." This striking image encapsulates the nature of projective verse as an imitation of life itself. As matter in space expands and collapses in the nova, so too does life expand and then dwindle in us. As a whole, however, the poem envisions energy as a continuum and connects that energy with a positive, searching, womanly power.

Caroline Herschel is a woman and a monster/witch, yet she discovered eight comets. She was not frozen into space, "doing penance for impetousness." She used her "eye, / virile, precise and absolutely certain." Rich's use of "virile" contrasts Herschel's success in overcoming any masculine/feminine split within herself and the fate of "galaxies of women." Their "impetuousness . . . chilled" not in outer space but in their own minds, many women place in exile the virile qualities that drove Herschel to her discoveries. Rich's theme is powerlessness versus power, particularly that of women who deny the virile in themselves for fear of being called monster: a "truly female" woman does not exhibit so-called "masculine" traits. Four years later, in 1972, Rich addresses this issue of sexual identity in her essay "The Antifeminist Woman." She writes that "it is easy to say we cannot ever know what is truly male or truly female. There is much we can know. We do know that these principles have been split apart and set in antagonism within each of us by a male-dominated intellectual and political heritage" (*On Lies, Secrets, and Silence*, p. 78). In "Planetarium" Rich overcomes that split by depicting a woman like Herschel.

She does not, however, limit her meaning to women, as we

learn from lines 24–25, which take us back to the sixteenth century and to Tycho, the astronomer-builder of the Uranusborg observatory. In the present of the poem he is "whispering at last / 'Let me not have lived in vain.'" A similar desire preoccupies Adrienne Rich. Her route, however, is not through the stars but through the power of poetry. The remainder of the poem explores the nature of that power:

> What we see, we see
> and seeing is changing
>
> the light that shrivels a mountain
> and leaves a man alive
>
> Heartbeat of the pulsar
> heart sweating through my body
>
> The radio impulse
> pouring in from Taurus
>
>   I am bombarded yet   I stand
>
> I have been standing all my life in the
> direct path of a battery of signals
> the most accurately transmitted most
> untranslatable language in the universe
> I am a galactic cloud so deep   so invo-
> luted that a light wave could take 15
> years to travel through me   And has
> taken   I am an instrument in the shape
> of a woman trying to translate pulsations
> into images   for the relief of the body
> and the reconstruction of the mind.

In the first section, unstated connections between the couplets form the flow of energy: the aesthetic power of the poem. The initial statement constitutes a touchstone for the others, all of which are images of waves of energy in one form or another. For example, the "heartbeat of the pulsar" would be a light wave, while the "heart sweating through my body" would be a wave of blood. Between them, an unstated connection. Then, of course, a radio wave is contained in the "impulse / pouring in from Taurus." Primarily tactile, these waves of energy constitute an additional way of "seeing." However we "see" the connections between the universe and us, the poem says we are bound to change our perception. Power resides in the seeing that enlarges our sense of the life-force: the same in us as in the magnitude of the nova.

Is seeing changing? Caroline Herschel saw the nova and changed our sense of the nature of the universe. Adrienne Rich sees Caroline Herschel and compares her with other women. She sees the heartbeat of the pulsar and feels the heartbeat in her own body. She sees, that is, what poets see: the universe in a grain of sand, a blade of grass. Observation leads to action: she must transmit what she sees. Women may allow themselves to be trapped by their sense of femininity; they may deny their "virile" eyes. Or, they may accept what is virile in them. As the last section of the poem indicates, Rich accepts what is virile in her—her male poet, her animus. "The radio impulse / pouring in from Taurus" the bull recalls the bull image from "The Demon Lover" in *Leaflets*. In that poem, the speaker felt how "the old wine pours again through my veins," as in "Orion" she had felt that "old transfusion." Both images carried sexual connotations. The emphasis here is different: "I am bombarded   yet I stand." The spacing that indicates the pause of the poet's breath as she would speak the line allows the last part of the line to stand apart—as the speaker stands, whole, integral. Her back is not against the wall, nor does she collapse in ennui. She is strong.

While the reference to Taurus brings in the element of the male animus, sexual response in the old way is not a factor in "Planetarium." In the last lines Rich retains her sense of being a woman while she takes on the function of the poet. The poem begins with the image of "A woman in the shape of a monster" and ends with the image of "an instrument in the shape / of a woman." The shift in the imagery indicates a reorientation of the poet's mind. Not simply a personal, subjective self, the "I" in the poem becomes a transmitter of energy, "trying to translate pulsations / into images for the relief of the body / and the reconstruction of the mind." Not only her body and mind, but *the* body and *the* mind. In effect, this poem takes as its purpose the transference of power, a womanly power, beneficent and healing. Through its use of speech rhythms, its handling of metaphor and tenses, "Planetarium" fulfills the criteria for projective verse—the vehicle of that transference.

Rich's sense of her own power as a poet is reinforced in "I Dream I'm the Death of Orpheus" (1968), a modern reshaping of the myth of Orpheus in the underworld. Taking its images from the Jean Cocteau film (*ARP*, p. 147), Rich's poem is overtly feminist and carries forth her theme of the "reconstruction of the mind." In this poem, her psyche undergoes the changes. In reading the poem, we participate in this reconstruction and observe how Rich transforms the myth to suit her own purposes.

In the myth the poet-singer Orpheus goes to the underworld to beg for the return of his beloved wife Eurydice. Pluto and Proserpine are moved by his plea but stipulate that Eurydice must walk behind him as the reunited couple leaves. The gods also exact his promise not to look back. Unable to control his fear and love for her, he turns around and she is swept back to the underworld. He must return alone to the land of the living. In this myth Orpheus represents the hero and his journey from the conscious (upper) world to the lower world. Eurydice, the beloved woman, resides in the world of the unconscious. She is essentially passive while Orpheus is the active agent undertaking the heroic struggle. When he fails, he learns he must obey the whim of the gods, no matter how arbitrary.

Rich's poem transforms this myth and puts it into a modern, feminist iconography:

> I am walking rapidly through striations of light and dark
> thrown under an arcade.
>
> I am a woman in the prime of life, with certain powers
> and those powers severely limited
> by authorities whose faces I rarely see.
> I am a woman in the prime of life
> driving her dead poet in a black Rolls-Royce
> through a landscape of twilight and thorns.
> A woman with a certain mission
> which if obeyed to the letter will leave her intact.

A woman with the nerves of a panther
a woman with contacts among Hell's Angels
a woman feeling the fullness of her powers
at the precise moment when she must not use them
a woman sworn to lucidity
who sees through the mayhem, the smoky fires
of these underground streets
her dead poet learning to walk backward against the wind
on the wrong side of the mirror

First, the heroic protagonist is a woman "in the prime of life, with certain powers." She has assumed the role of Orpheus and the title of the poem thus becomes a pun: she *is* the death of Orpheus because she usurps his power. The female hero, an active agent, rescues the passive, *dead* poet. He is her animus; she is bringing him back to life. Just as Orpheus in the myth was ordered to behave in a certain fashion by the gods of the underworld, so too Rich's heroic female is "severely limited / by authorities whose faces I rarely see." Operating under constraint, she proceeds through difficult terrain, albeit in an elegant "black Rolls-Royce." Rich modernizes the myth with such an image. Similarly modern is her handling of the heroic bragging motif: she has "the nerves of a panther" and "contacts among Hell's Angels."

Her greatest act of heroism is to experience "the fullness of her powers / at the precise moment when she must not use them." Unlike Orpheus, she succeeds despite her constraints. The hero represents consciousness; likewise, this woman is "sworn to lucidity" and can "see through the mayhem." In true mythic fashion she makes a descent to the "underground," the realm of the unconscious, and returns to the conscious state with her resurrected animus. In writing the poem (recording the dream), she achieves psychic integration. The poem ends on a positive note, for we discover "her dead poet learning to walk backwards against the wind," not passive anymore but active and savvy. If he is on "the wrong side of the mirror," it is only because the speaker is looking into the mirror and seeing the animus/poet in her reflection.

As Albert Gelpi points out in his article "Adrienne Rich: the Poetics of Change," "Selfhood is the motive and end of the journey" (*ARP*, p. 147). For the author of "Planetarium" and "I Dream I'm the Death of Orpheus," the reenactment of this psychic journey takes on an added dimension signified by her use of myth. Gelpi explains the significance of myth in Rich's poetry:

> The fact that hers is not merely a private struggle but a summons to us all—at least to all of us who enter the door and cross the threshold into the psyche—informs the poetry with a mythic dimension in a singularly demythologized time. A myth not because her experience has been appended, by literary allusion, to gods and goddesses, but because her experience is rendered so deeply and truly that it reaches common impulses and springs, so that, without gods and goddesses, we can participate in the process of discovery and determination. It is existentialism raised to a mythic power, and the myth has personal and political implications. The result is a restoration to poetry of an ancient and primitive power, lost in the crack-up which the last centuries have documented. The power of the bard in his tribe has long since declined with the power of prophecy. Adrienne Rich's mission is to live out her dream of a society of individual men and women. By challenging us to a more honest realization, she has recovered something of the function of the poet among his people: not by transmitting their legends and tales but by offering herself—without pretensions, with honest hesitations—as the mirror of their consciousness and the medium of their transformation. (*ARP*, pp. 147–48)

Significant as well is that Rich assumes the role of the bard among *her* people. As a woman who dares to transcend patriarchal barriers in becoming this "bard," Rich enacts a transformation that is personal, poetic, and political. Rich can, therefore, become a model for us; her courage, her personal honesty, and her achievement are estimable. "Shooting Script," a more extended mythic journey, provides a deeper sense of the nature of that achievement.

"Shooting Script," the second section of the volume, displays an extended use of myth, both in the ordinary sense of a psychic journey and in the terms in which that myth is rendered. The psychic journey tells a tale of purposeful destruction that culminates in the creation of a new order for the poet. The willfulness of this destruction makes some of Rich's critics uncomfortable. Robert Boyers, for one, finds "the will to change" nothing but an "ideological fashion" and Rich a less remarkable poet for adopting it. It has turned her, he says, "from wholeness to analytic lucidity." Boyers objects, therefore, to Rich's stance and not necessarily to the fragmented form of her verse. For him, Rich's poems in this volume lack "a poised maturity." His most serious charge is that Rich "has ceased to be herself, that blend of instinct and learned wisdom, innocent eye and educated adult, who knew there was a limit to will, and worth in steadfastness" (*ARP*, pp. 159–60). Boyers may be right in detecting the incipient ideologue in Rich's making such a conscious choice to become other than what she has been. But if her aesthetic is radical rather than "steadfast," it comes from her experience in a world profoundly inimical to her assertion of powerful womanliness, where a woman such as Adrienne Rich is a "monster." Groping and supremely disoriented, the poetic consciousness in "Shooting Script" goes through an intense period of confusion and fragmentation in an attempt both to destroy and to reconstruct itself. Traditional forms will not serve her; she must allow herself to be influenced differently, this time by the cinema.

As the title "Shooting Script" asserts, these poems are not the finished product—not the movie. Rich follows through, then, on what she says in "Images for Godard": "the notes for the poem are the only poem." The influence of Olson and his theory of projective verse can also be heard in Rich's assertions. Her aesthetic depends upon a kind of indeterminacy that Olson would applaud. She *will not* create any polished form; she will do away with "form" in the old sense—and work with her "notes."

Like a set of notes, "Shooting Script" has a raw, unfinished quality, and the majority of the poems depend for their effect upon fragmentation. Segments may be one to four lines long with no emphasis upon subtlety of line break. Where the margins come, the line is broken. Rich's proselike lineation does not aim for the tension of her typical line breaks. Likewise, stress patterns are nonexistent. Segmentation and interval are the sole determinants of form. Rich's technique can best be described by a portion of the fifth poem in the sequence: "Evenings at table, turning the findings out, pushing them / around with a finger, beginning to dream of fitting them together." The parts of the poem, then, are like the pieces of a jigsaw puzzle. The action of the poet is to move these pieces around freely, her juxtapositions arbitrary yet reflective.

"Shooting Script" is, therefore, a difficult poem to read and appreciate: its form is fragmented, so too is the psyche of the poet. Either we say, "Forget it. I want poems that make more sense and that don't demand so much faith on my part that the poet knows what she's doing." Or we become active readers, following Rich into the confusion and seeming disorder, so that we can participate in "the reconstruction of the mind." Hers or ours, it does not matter. She becomes our scapegoat, if we will let her. Our reading of these poems—despite our prejudices for "form" and artistic control—becomes a willful act. While we cannot will our liking a work of art, we can exert a will to understand an artist's attempt to discover new forms.

Rich's poetic *script* is divided into two sections and there are fourteen poems altogether. Poem 8 illustrates the cinematic quality of Rich's style. Essentially a poem about loneliness, separation, and estrangement, this poem has a simple set, a bedroom, and a single actor—a woman poet waking up on a winter morning. Consider the first five elements in the script:

A woman waking behind grimed blinds slatted across a courtyard she never looks into.

Thinking of the force of a waterfall, the slash of cold air from the thickest water of the falls, slicing the green and ochre afternoon in which he turns his head and walks away.

Thinking of that place as an existence.

A woman reaching for the glass of water left all night on the bureau, the half-done poem, the immediate relief.

Entering the poem as a method of leaving the room.

Obviously, the cinematic motif takes the poet only so far: a camera would have difficulty filming the third unit above. With her words, the poet can name her persona's inner state. Further on, for example, she writes: "The woman is too heavy for the poem, she is a swollenness, a foot / an arm, gone asleep, grown absurd and out of bounds." As the woman cannot put herself into the poem, the poet resists shaping her material (a sensation, an action, a thought, a fantasy) into a finished product or object of art. Thus Rich's technique demands that the reader "finish" the poem. While she writes the script, we create the "movie" in our minds by assembling the various shots. If "the moment of change is the only poem," Rich makes possible that moment through the intervals between "shots" in her cinematic "shooting script."

Juxtapositions are extremely arbitrary in the opening sections of "Shooting Script," as can be illustrated by the first five lines of poem 1:

We were bound on the wheel of an endless conversation.

Inside this shell, a tide waiting for someone to enter.

A monologue waiting for you to interrupt it.

A man wades into the surf. The dialogue of the rock with the breaker.

The wave changed instantly by the rock; the rock changed by the wave returning over and over.

Rich's images turn upon desire for communication: shell to tide, rock to breaker, person to person. All are obsessive: "the endless conversation," the "wave returning over and over." The effect of such a poem is innovative patterning like that of a montage. Cinematically, a montage is a rapid sequence of thematically related short scenes or images. At its best, Rich's script achieves that rapid flow. At its worst, "Shooting Script" generates a chaotic verbal rambling. By adopting the poem-montage as a technique, Rich does away with traditional discourse—its continuity, order, reasonable progression, and sequence. She does away with logic and "sense."

The cinematic influence upon "Shooting Script" is surrealist, the conventions of which have been present—to a certain degree—in Rich's poetry since *Leaflets*. Purposeful fragmentation, the surrender to chance, and the arbitrary were key elements in the 1969 volume. In *The Will to Change*, her use of surrealist conventions grows more extensive. For example, in many of these poems, her persona is often a sleepwalker in the tradition of surrealist narrative where the somnambulist wanders through a dreamscape. In the ninth poem of the series, she writes about "stumbling / through the darkness, finding my place among the sleepers and / masturbators in the dark." This image also refers, of course, to entering a darkened movie theater. In poem 6, she writes of a similar movement through a dark space: "You are beside me like a wall. I touch you with my fingers and keep moving through the bad light." Rich uses a somnambulist persona in order to maximize her chances of "restructuring the mind." For her, this involves the same quest as that of *Necessities of Life* and *Leaflets:* to bring more of the shadow energies into her poetry, thus effecting union with the "dark" side of the self.

The dreams the somnambulist enters are fragmentary—as is the form of Rich's verse. This, too, is a key aspect of surrealism, described as "a late variant of Romantic taste, a Romanticism that assumes a broken or posthumous world reflecting the buried psychological or collective realities. Surrealist works proceed by conventions of dismemberment and reconstitution."[4] That is, purposeful fragmentation moves toward a new kind of order.

In certain key poems, the pieces begin to fit together in coherent patterns. As more and more pieces begin to cohere, there is a gradual, painful coming together that speaks of the psychic reintegration of the poet. Power is involved in all of this, not simply as a theme, but in the very *act* of what Rich accomplishes in "Shooting Script." She destroys in order to create; there lies the power of the poet. Poem 6 from part 1 of "Shooting Script" clarifies some of these matters and brings the issue of power into sharper focus.

In poem 6, the speaker journeys along a frontier. Difficulty arises in negotiating the trail: the light is bad. Unable to see very well, the speaker nonetheless keeps moving. Fortunately, another person stands "beside me like a wall." This other person—the *you* in the poem—is herself. Poem 7 tells us this: "when the change leaves you dark . . . when I thought I prayed, when I was talking to myself under the cover of my darkness." The journey through the dark becomes the journey of the hero on the path to psychic reintegration. Such a quest demands a relinquishment of the powers of consciousness. When the speaker's powerlessness does not enervate her, her sense of the nature of power undergoes change.

Cyclical in structure, the poem's beginning is its ending, the binding quality of repetition counteracting the poem's fragmentation and discontinuity:

> You are beside me like a wall; I touch you with my fingers and keep moving through the bad light.
>
> At this time of year when faces turn aside, it is amazing that your eyes are to be met.
>
> A bad light is one like this, that flickers and diffuses itself along the edge of a frontier.
>
> No, I don't invest you with anything; I am counting on your weakness as much as on your strength.
>
> This light eats away at the clarities I had fixed on; it moves up like a rodent at the edge of the raked paths.
>
> Your clarities may not reach me; but your attention will.
>
> It is to know that I too have no mythic powers; it is to see the liability of all my treasures.

You will have to see all this for a long time alone.

You are beside me like a wall; I touch you with my fingers
and keep trying to move through the bad light.

Ironically, the imagery of the poem moves toward greater accuracy. This can be seen in Rich's handling of the "bad light." At
first simply part of the atmosphere—"I . . . keep moving
through the bad light"—it assumes more significance in line 3,
where it is *defined* by means of its function. It "flickers and dif-
fuses itself along the edge of a frontier." Even this is inadequate.
In line 5, Rich charges the light image with one of the major
themes of this volume: it "eats away at the clarities I had fixed
on; it moves up / like a rodent at the edge of the raked paths."
The "clarities" are the "raked paths"; both signify the old order.
Destructive and repellent, the "rodent" eats away at the old
order, signifying in its action the power to destroy. Countering
the destruction of the old clarities, the pinpoint accuracy of
Rich's language calls the new order into being.

Nonetheless, Rich surrenders her conception of her own superiority: "I too have no mythic powers." What she discovers in
the bad light is "the liability of all my treasures." From other
things she has said in this volume and from the direction her
poetry has taken away from traditional forms, her "treasures"
include traditional ways of seeing. Mind consciousness heads
the list. The ability to think, to reason clearly, to formulate
ideas, to draw logical conclusions—all here, all valued most
highly. But, of what value are such qualities in "bad light"?
Where one cannot see to think, one must feel. That is why touch
predominates in this poem. With "fingers" not eyes she will effect a transfer of her "powers," becoming in the process more
vulnerable, more human. Maybe she cannot change the world,
but she can touch another person. Maybe she cannot see too
well, but she keeps moving through the bad light supported by
the "you." In contrast to "Orion"—that poem of existential
angst—she does not have her back to the wall nor is she alone.
Her posture has changed; the wall has changed. No longer static
in her power, she moves and "You are beside me like a wall." She

needs support; she gets it. She knows her weakness and "counts" on it.

As stated previously, Adrienne Rich's sense of her power changes. Most important, she does not value anymore power that is invulnerable, cold, and distant. Her movement away from such a valuation can be observed in the shift that occurs in her imagery, in particular the wall image. A comparable shift occurs in her use of the shadow. In the darkness of the poem's atmosphere, the "you" becomes the shadow-self. No longer abnegated or merely longed for as in *Leaflets*, this shadow-self takes a closer position to the poet—and vice versa. The emergence of this shadow-self and the intimacy of the relationship between the *I* and the *you* indicate that Rich has accomplished her desire to change.

Poem 13, next to the last in "Shooting Script," climaxes that accomplishment and recapitulates Rich's themes. It is night; the persona departs in a boat. She is probably dreaming. As in surrealist narrative, this poem concerns surrender to chance and to the arbitrary:

> We are driven to odd attempts; once it would not have
> occurred to me to put out in a boat, not on a night like this.
>
> Still, it was an instrument, and I had pledged myself to try
> any instrument that came my way. Never to refuse one from
> conviction of incompetence.
>
> A long time I was simply learning to handle the skiff; I had
> no special training and my own training was against me.
>
> I had always heard that darkness and water were a threat.
>
> In spite of this, darkness and water helped me to arrive here.
>
> I watched the lights on the shore I had left for a long time;
> each one, it seemed to me, was a light I might have lit, in the
> old days.

In this beautifully rendered poem, surrender to chance dominates both the boat metaphor and thematic statement: "We are driven to odd attempts" and "I had pledged myself to try any instrument that came my way" and "darkness and water helped me to arrive here." The poet does not name the place where she has arrived. Primarily, it is an awareness of competency. She has created her own order, "having been driven to odd attempts" like the innovative forms of "Shooting Script," like "restructuring the mind." She is strong because she does not allow her "conviction of incompetence" to keep her from her quest. Unlike the ordinary hero, she possesses no superhuman qualities and her "own training" becomes her antagonist rather than her armor in the struggle. Like the hero, she enters the "darkness and water" converting them from a "threat" to the ground of her transformation. Heroically, she goes from the light to darkness: "I watched the lights on the shore I had left for a long time." Her journey, however, is incomplete.

Poem 14 finishes the journey and this volume. The shooting script has served its purpose: she has found what she was looking for—or it has found her. Early in the volume, she writes in "Study of History":

> . . . after
> all we have never entirely
> known what was done to you upstream
> what powers trepanned
> which of your channels diverted

At the end of the volume, her quest complete, she *knows* "what powers [were] trepanned," but she is deliberately vague about the nature of her findings:

> Whatever it was: the grains of the glacier caked in the boot-cleats; ashes spilled on white formica.
>
> The death-col viewed through power-glasses; the cube of ice melting on stainless steel.
>
> Whatever it was, the image that stopped you, the one on which you came to grief, projecting it over & over on empty walls.

Her vagueness about what she has seen is emphasized by the repetition of "whatever it was." In the first three segments she makes the point that her awareness could have been achieved in a variety of ways. The speaker only knows that something has stopped her and she keeps looking at it over and over again.

The image could be something large and outside the self, as "The death-col viewed through power-glasses." Or it could be something trivial and domestic: "the cube of ice melting on stainless steel." This poem, therefore, validates Rich's technique. In the home movie, the scope and variety of the images have allowed the speaker to see "the image . . . the one on which you came to grief." Now that her movie is finished, she can "give up the temptations of the projector."

Stopped by that image—"whatever it was"—the speaker concentrates on the *ground* of that "on which you came to grief." The rest of the poem proceeds in ghazal-like couplets, each beginning with an infinitive:

> To read there the map of the future, the roads radiating from
> the initial split, the filaments thrown out from that impasse.
>
> To reread the instructions on your palm; to find there how
> the lifeline, broken, keeps its direction.
>
> To read the etched rays of the bullet-hole left years ago in the
> glass; to know in every distortion of the light what fracture is.
>
> To put the prism in your pocket, the thin glass lens, the map
> of the inner city, the little book with gridded pages.
>
> To pull yourself up by your own roots; to eat the last meal in
> your old neighborhood.

The infinitive phrases not only provide a syntactic uniformity to the couplets, but they also convey the sense of action going on at the present time—the immediacy and intensity of Rich's resolve. Further unifying the poem, giving it order and coherence, is the image pattern initiated by "the web of cracks filtering across the plaster." Such is the ground of the image "on which you came to grief"—the one which "trepanned" your powers.

All these images concern something damaged: "the initial split," the "broken lifeline," the "rays of the bullet-hole." In essence, this image cluster leads naturally to the central metaphor of her next book of poems, *Diving into the Wreck*. In that volume, she makes clear the nature of the wreck, the damage: that is, the split between male and female—not just "the war between the sexes," but the taboo that denies the integration of the male and female in the individual human psyche. Before she dives into the wreck, she will exchange the tools she names above: "the prism" and "the map of the inner city" for the more serviceable knife and camera. In the quality of its image patterns, therefore, the last poem in *The Will to Change* anticipates dominant motifs in Rich's next book of poems.

In *The Will to Change*, Adrienne Rich's task is to bring about "the relief of the body and the reconstruction of the mind." She accomplishes this for herself. This "instrument in the shape of a woman" possesses the power-to-transform and would like to transmit this energy from herself to her audience. Under the influence of Charles Olson's poetic theory, she experiments with different strategies in her poems to reenact the energy constructs required by projective verse. This reenactment leads her into the territory of myth and she becomes, for us, the hero—a symbol of transformation.

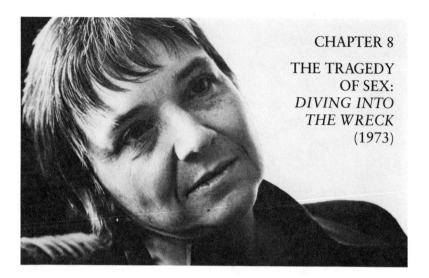

CHAPTER 8

THE TRAGEDY
OF SEX:
*DIVING INTO
THE WRECK*
(1973)

ON THE JACKET COVER of *Diving into the Wreck*, Adrienne Rich describes how she sees the poems in this volume. To her, they are:

> A coming-home to the darkest and richest sources of my poetry: sex, sexuality, sexual wounds, sexual identity, sexual politics: many names for pieces of one whole. I feel this book continues the work I've been trying to do—breaking down the artificial barriers between private and public, between Vietnam and the lovers' bed, between the deepest images we carry out of our dreams and the most daylight events "out in the world." This is the intention and longing behind everything I write.

Rich's sense of herself as a sexual being—a woman who has been wounded—assumes the utmost importance in this volume. Because she is a feminist, she regards her sexuality as part of a larger fabric of sexual politics, that is, male domination. Rich's concern with these issues gives shape to the nature of her poetry, its tones, themes, images, and audience. What emerges is an angry feminist voice.

Rich is angry at men, and some of her most striking poems

emerge from this anger. In "The Phenomenology of Anger," for example, she writes:

> . . . When I dream of meeting
> the enemy, this is my dream:
>
> white acetylene
> ripples from my body
> effortlessly released
> perfectly trained
> on the true enemy
>
> raking his body down to the thread
> of existence
> burning away his lie
> leaving him in a new
> world; a changed
> man

Although the impulse of this passage is toward transformation, the stance of the speaker is authoritarian, convinced of its rightness and the man's "lie." Later on, in one of the most poignant lines of the volume, a note of self-doubt enters: "If I am death to man / I have to know it." It almost seems as if one side of Rich (gentle, caring, nurturant) does not know the other: the man-hater. In general, Rich's attitude toward men in this volume is peremptory; she has given up understanding men or sympathizing with them.

It is difficult to imagine, therefore, a male audience for such poems or a female audience of "male-identified" women. Either Rich denigrates men or she ignores them; her allegiance is with women. The audience for these poems would have to be pro-feminist and moving toward female identification, that is, women who derive their primary identity from an integral womanhood and not from their relationships with men. In many of her poems, Rich draws on elements women have in common: experiences such as giving birth, a certain biology, particular kinds of fantasies and dreams. When she assumes a female audience with certain shared realities, she brings a heightened focus to her poetry. Even when she addresses a man her subject is woman's experience. In this volume, Adrienne Rich's sense of community with women galvanizes her energies and gives her poetry the same kind of "charge" we find in Sylvia Plath's. Like Plath, Rich is nervy and daring, but her stance is more deeply committed to a radical politics.

When Rich adopts a radical, feminist stance that will not allow any qualification, she becomes an ideologue. Thus she writes with calm assurance: "everything outside our skins is an image / of this affliction." While there is much truth in her ideology (men can be beasts; women have been oppressed by men), she is an extremist and her total view leads to the absurdity of the poem "The Ninth Symphony of Beethoven Understood at Last as a Sexual Message." In *Diving into the Wreck,* Rich regards men as nihilistic and masculinity as "spreading impotence upon the world." Part of her revulsion toward men is conditioned by her sexual reorientation toward women. She becomes a lover of women, which is a subtext of the volume. There is something waiting to be born in women and Rich loves this incipience. In the poem "Incipience," she contrasts women and men in a scenario that encapsulates her views about the life-negating fatalism of the male and the idealism and sisterhood of women:

A man is asleep in the next room
    He has spent a whole day
    standing, throwing stones into the black pool
    which keeps its blackness
Outside the frame of his dream we are stumbling up the
    hill   hand in hand, stumbling and guiding each other
    over the scarred volcanic rock

Even though Rich's female identification is evident in *Diving into the Wreck* in poems such as the one above, she still feels drawn by some old thinking, specifically toward the concept of androgyny. For example, she says in "The Stranger," "I am the androgyne," meaning that she combines within herself both masculine and feminine traits. Since Rich excoriates men and masculinity relentlessly in *Diving into the Wreck,* it is difficult to understand why or how she could incorporate maleness into her womanhood. Even so, Rich holds onto an androgynous ideal, the subject of her title poem, "Diving into the Wreck." This poem presents a vision of a male/female fantasy creature who would transcend the inadequacies of both sexes. The thrust of the book as a whole rejects the synthesis of masculine and feminine that its title poem suggests. Rich's ultimate allegiance is with her womanhood. This allegiance, however, is not fully realized by the poet and makes for a problematic volume of poetry that is clearly transitional.

Rich's sense of community with women was fostered in her, as in many other women, by the second stage of the women's movement. Her awareness of this community goes back to her *Snapshots of a Daughter-in-Law*. In the middle and late sixties, her political activism evolved into a concern for women's issues and to a love for women. She embraced feminist ideology and became a spokesperson for the movement. Granted the National Book Award for *Diving into the Wreck* in 1974, she accepted it along with Audre Lorde and Alice Walker, two other nominees, in the name of all women:

> We . . . together accept this award in the name of all the women whose voices have gone and still go unheard in a patriarchal world, and in the name of those who, like us, have been tolerated as token women in this culture, often at great personal cost and in great pain. . . . We symbolically join here in refusing the terms of patriarchal competition and declaring that we will share this prize among us, to be used as best we can for women. . . . We dedicate this occasion to the struggle for self-determination of all women, of every color, identification or derived class . . . the women who will understand what we are doing here and those who will not understand yet; the silent women whose voices have been denied us, the articulate women who have given us strength to do our work. (*ARP*, p. 204)

Rich's bountiful idealism is extremely moving. When she embraced the feminist cause, she gave birth to a powerful rhetoric. With Lorde and Walker, Rich recognizes that women are at various levels of consciousness. The urgency of *Diving into the*

Wreck comes, in part, from the dialectic between Rich's speakers and other women who have not been "driven to odd attempts." Primarily, the poet wants to develop in other women what she has developed in herself: a sense of womanly power different from the kind of power that has resulted in the wreck of civilization that she sees all about her.

This womanly power is personal in that it depends upon the development of individual strength and vitality in a woman. It is transformative in that it involves change within the woman concerning certain societal notions about feminine passivity and submission. Essential to the development of this personal power is bonding among women, which will generate a political power capable of making changes on a larger scale, among them a radical shift in the power structures of the patriarchy. In *Diving into the Wreck*, Rich renders these ideas about womanly power in some of her strongest poems to date.

Concerned with sexual politics, these poems culminate Rich's development from the "modest" poet of her first book of poems to the quiet but steady subversive of her second. When she articulated the complaints of "Snapshots of a Daughter-in-Law," she prepared us for the poetry of "visionary anger" we encounter in *Diving into the Wreck*. If she is "fierce," as Cheryl Walker in her review of this volume says (*Reading Adrienne Rich*, p. 228), then she has learned from her female, poetic forbears. Like Emily Dickinson, she is having it out "on her own premises"—those of a feminist radical, dedicated to challenging the assumptions of the patriarchy.

In her essay "The Anti-Feminist Woman," written at the same time as many of the poems in this book, Rich defines both patriarchy and the feminist position. By patriarchy she means "any kind of group organization in which males hold dominant power and determine what part females shall and shall not play, and in which capabilities assigned to women are relegated generally to the mystical and aesthetic and excluded from the practical and political realms" (*ARP*, p. 101). Based on the subjugation of women and of the feminine, patriarchal power can be defined as the power-to-control. Adrienne Rich writes "of a world masculinity made unfit for women or men" in her poem "Merced." This "unfit world" is one of the meanings of the wreck her persona dives into, trying "to find the damage that was done / and the treasures that prevail." As a radical, Rich wants to get back to the root and hopefully find the source of power-that-does-not-destroy. For her, that power is located in women.

Beginning with her sense of what it means to be a woman, her poems reach out to encompass many facets of American life—our culture, history, customs, daily rituals, news from the war front in Vietnam, city life, vacations in Yosemite, movies, dreams. She places all these matters in the total perspective of sexual politics and the power of the patriarchy. Within the patriarchal system, woman is a marginal figure, capable of seeing, Rich believes, what men in power cannot see because women do not participate in the kingdom of the fathers. Neither do most men. Yet Rich's vision does not encompass any qualifications. Her explorations into sexual politics bring her to the conclusion that all men are guilty of crimes against women and against life on this planet. Even the protectors are the enemy, as in "Rape," where the neighborhood cop is regarded as a mirror image of the rapist. "I trust none of them," the speaker declares in "For a Sister." At the end of the volume, Rich quotes a mother's admonition to her daughters, *Men can do things to you.* The crimes of men extend from the individual rape of one woman to more universal devastation:

> I suddenly see the world
> as no longer viable:
> you are out there burning the crops
> with some new sublimate
> This morning you left the bed
> we still share
> and went out to spread impotence
> upon the world

In this selection from "The Phenomenology of Anger," Rich makes the connection between man's relationship to women and his violation of nature. In her vision the two are linked.[1] Rich's indictment of the patriarchy develops into a sweeping universality. There are no more fragments. Whereas *Leaflets* and *The Will to Change* developed an aesthetic based upon fragmentation and disunity, *Diving into the Wreck* pulls all the pieces together into a coherent whole.

The "one whole" Rich postulates may be repugnant to many who do not or cannot see all men as the enemy. Nonetheless, Rich's poetry derives its power from the inclusiveness of her aesthetic. All facets of life are subsumed in a radical feminist vision that names the exaggerated forms of masculinity as the evil and the development of a personal/political female power as the good. Rich's own poetry achieves that power to the extent that she develops a female aesthetic. This aesthetic emerges in poems that validate a female imagery, speak in a woman's voice, and urge the utterance of woman's "unsaid word." In this last respect, Rich condemns the lies women speak in defense of male superiority, the secrets women hold within that keep them from developing a female community, and the silences that deny and may even negate a woman's full emergence into a power that would be a beneficent counterforce to male power. Fittingly, Rich's 1979 collection of selected prose, *On Lies, Secrets, and Silence*, echoes these same concerns.

Rich's opening poem begins to develop her idea of a womanly power that is distinct from her idea of masculine power. "Trying to Talk with a Man" establishes the connection between private and public life in a striking and poignant allegory. Line 1 announces the basic motif of the poem—"Out in this desert we are testing bombs"—and sets up the narrative. In effect, the political climate of the nuclear age provides Adrienne Rich with metaphors for the disjunctions in the relationship between a man and a woman. The woman speaker of the poem makes her stance clear: the war between the sexes is at the core of the larger, political shambles. The "deformed cliffs" of the desert and its "condemned scenery" suggest the ruin of a civilization intent on destroying itself. The man and the woman in the landscape of the poem have several options: build more effective bombs, exit by committing suicide, or discover the cause of the destruction. As the movement of the poem indicates, that cause lies in the breakdown of the relationship between the sexes—a breakdown attributable to their different notions of power.

For the woman, power exists in the connection between her physical being and the natural world, a bond that evolves into the clarification of feelings and perceptions and the development of understanding. In the third line of the poem, the woman's state of feeling breaks into the external reality of the narrative:

> Out in this desert we are testing bombs,
>
> that's why we came here.
>
> Sometimes I feel an underground river
> forcing its way between deformed cliffs
> an acute angle of understanding
> moving itself like a locus of the sun
> into this condemned scenery.

After the starkness of the opening line and the redundancy of line 2, lines 3–7 move into the woman's awareness of the "underground river"—inside her and in the desert as well. The image suggests a birth passage whose difficulty is conveyed by the relationship of the "river / forcing its way between deformed cliffs" as a child along the birth canal. The sun as metaphor for the understanding within the speaker places her apart from the destruction. Not a destroyer, she is the mother of light, her power the creative power of sun and earth.

Rich clarifies her theme of regeneracy and woman's physicality in *Of Woman Born: Motherhood as Experience and Institution*, a prose work she was researching and writing during this same period. In her first chapter she makes the following declaration:

> I have come to believe, as will be clear throughout this book, that female biology—the diffuse, intense sensuality radiating out from clitoris, breasts, uterus, vagina; the lunar cycles of menstruation; the gestation and fruition of life which can take place in the female body—has far more radical implications than we have yet come to appreciate. Patriarchal thought has limited female biology to its

140

own narrow specifications. The feminist vision has recoiled from female biology for these reasons; it will, I believe, come to view our physicality as a resource, rather than a destiny. In order to live a fully human life we require not only *control* of our bodies (though control is a prerequisite); we must touch the unity and resonance of our physicality, our bond with the natural order, the corporeal ground of our intelligence. (p. 21)

In Rich's thought, woman's vital connection with Nature gives the female sex a distinct advantage in healing the mind-body split, the curse of modern, technological existence. Woman, as Rich's thinking goes, has more of a chance to accomplish that healing because of her "bond with the natural order." "Trying to Talk with a Man" renders this insight in poetic form.

The female speaker contrasts sharply with the man she addresses. Though she is aware of regenerative forces within, he concerns himself with the destructive forces outside—including the woman. A drain upon the woman's energy, he appears paranoid:

> Out here I feel more helpless
> with you than without you
> You mention the danger
> and list the equipment
> we talk of people caring for each other
> in emergencies—laceration, thirst—
> but you look at me like an emergency
>
> Your dry heat feels like power
> your eyes are stars of a different magnitude
> they reflect lights that spell out: EXIT
> when you get up and pace the floor
>
> talking of the danger
> as if it were not ourselves
> as if we were testing anything else.

In the last three lines Rich's speaker reinforces the "one whole" of the volume. The woman reminds the man that he is projecting "the danger" outside of himself: he regards political realities as the threat. Not so, the woman says; the danger is "ourselves."

The personal is the political. The curious simile "You look at me like an emergency" reflects the man's paranoia and the speaker's recognition of his irrationality. The simile defies our expectations. Customarily a word with a human factor would complete the comparison; for example, "You look at me like a policeman." By depersonalizing the noun, Rich renders the simile ambivalent. He looks at her as if *she* were the emergency or—he looks at her and *his looking* is the emergency. Just as he fears her, so too must she beware of the danger he presents. This second meaning is reinforced by the following line: "Your dry heat feels like power." Weakening the assertion of his power, "feels like" maintains its illusory nature. "Dry heat" is not power; the "underground river" is. Furthermore, his heat is regressive, leading him to "EXIT." In contrast, the woman's power flows into and clarifies "this condemned scenery."

Knowing that Rich's husband, Alfred Conrad, committed suicide in 1970 adds another perspective to the reading of this poem. His death must have forced her to consider his possible motives and what it meant that she survived him. In the poem "From a Survivor" her imagined audience is her dead husband, although she keeps secret his name and the means of his death. In both these poems, the speaker's survival is determined by a womanly power that involves her subjectivity and her insistence on the reality and importance of her states of feeling. There is a subtext as well: unlike her husband, Rich is a poet who can find forms for her feelings and thus can render her "survival" more likely.

Even if her husband or the man in the poem were a poet, in this volume Rich does not find much that is life-enhancing in contemporary poetry by men. Their poetry, like the views of the man in her poem, reveals to Adrienne Rich "a deep pessimism and a fatalistic grief." In her 1971 essay "When We Dead Awaken," she sees the remedy for contemporary male poets and for men in general in their moving closer to woman's power: "Man will have to learn to gestate and give birth to his own subjectivity—something he has wanted woman to do for him. We can go on trying to talk to each other . . . but women can no longer be primarily mothers and muses for men: we have our own work cut out for us."[2] A poem of the same title as Rich's essay suggests the importance to her of Ibsen's play *When We Dead Awaken*. As in the play, the dead are women whose lives have been used by men; instead of developing their own "subjectivity," men have drained women. Rich deplores this use of women as "the tragedy of sex." The whole vision of *Diving into the Wreck* rests on this issue. The following poem, "Waking in the Dark," deepens this theme.

A long poem in five parts, "Waking in the Dark" begins with sections on the violence and contempt for life in the twentieth century ("the man from Bangladesh / walks starving / on the front page"). It ends with a dream and a wish: a dream of man and woman loving one another ("there is no dismay / we move together like underwater plants")—a wish that women and men could do something "actual" to make that dream happen. This poem becomes, then, the last call of an old belief for Adrienne Rich—the idea that women and men could work together to make a better world. In the total context of the book, particularly in consideration of poems like "Merced" and "Rape" that condemn men and masculinity, Rich's dream appears tainted. "Waking in the Dark," however, still takes as its directive finding out "where the split began."

In the middle of the poem, section 3 forms the nucleus of Rich's thought. The opening line, "The tragedy of sex," presents the idea that an extended metaphor advances into a modern allegory:

> The tragedy of sex
> lies around us, a woodlot
> the axes are sharpened for.
> The old shelters and huts
> stare through the clearing with a certain resolution
> —the hermit's cabin, the hunter's shack—
> scenes of masturbation
> and dirty jokes.
> A man's world. But finished.
> They themselves have sold it to the machines.

> I walk the unconscious forest,
> a woman dressed in old army fatigues
> that have shrunk to fit her, I am lost
> at moments, I feel dazed
> by the sun pawing between the trees,
> cold in the bog and lichen of the thicket.
> Nothing will save this. I am alone,
> kicking the last rotting logs
> with their strange smell of life, not death,
> wondering what on earth it all might have become.

"The tragedy of sex" is rendered metaphorically as "a woodlot" just waiting to be cut down. Obviously something natural and vital, sex becomes tragic when it is used in a perverse way, for "masturbation / and dirty jokes." Men are portrayed as degenerates whose rapaciousness has brought about the tragedy. The woman in the poem acts as a witness. Characteristically, she discovers the "strange smell of life" in the "unconscious forest," but it is too late for anything but speculation about what might have been. Because the male power-to-control subjugates both nature and the feminine, men must bear the heavy burden of guilt for the despoliation the woman sees all about her.

In sum, the poetic consciousness in these poems seeks not to assume man's power, but to develop a wholly different way of being in the world. To that end, Rich composes a series of poems in which her listener, the person whom she is addressing, is another woman. Among her poems written for a female audience are "When We Dead Awaken," parts of "Waking in the Dark," "Incipience," "After Twenty Years," "The Mirror in Which Two Are Seen as One," and "The Phenomenology of Anger." The tone in these poems is determined in large part by Rich's speaking to other women.

"When We Dead Awaken" is Rich's companion piece to "Trying to Talk with a Man" in that she is trying to talk with a woman, or with women in general. Its title comes from the Ibsen play that Rich describes as "about the use that the male artist and thinker—in the process of creating culture as we know it—

has made of women in his life and work; and about a woman's slow struggling awakening to the use to which her life has been put" (*ARP*, p. 90). The poem opens with "Trying to tell you how"—that is, its syntax is similar to the title of the first poem. The "you" in "When We Dead Awaken," Rich's imagined audience, is a woman who has not awakened yet to the truths known to Rich's speaker. Those truths come down to the "one whole" of this book—how man's domination of women is the primal fault that predetermines his disrespect and violation of nature: "everything outside our skins is an image / of this affliction." In the last section of part 1, Rich's imagined audience enters as "even you, fellow-creature, sister." She addresses this woman in incantatory lines that are part repetition of syntactic phrases, part catalog:

> everything outside my skin
> speaks of the fault that sends me limping
> even the scars of my decisions
> even the sunblaze in the mica-vein
> even you, fellow-creature, sister,
> sitting across from me, dark with love,
> working with me to pick apart
> working with me to remake
> this trailing knitted thing, this cloth of darkness,
> this woman's garment, trying to save the skein.

While Rich's terms of address are intimate, even familial, her persona adopts a superior position in regard to her listener. She knows more. The other woman is "dark with love," but the speaker cannot love that which is flawed—not even herself. She too has a "fault that sends me limping." Although disabled by her "fault," she can work with the other woman. The last two lines are an image of woman, which is itself female: "this trailing knitted thing." Together the women are trying to undo the damage that has been done to themselves. While man may indeed knit, this kind of needle-and-thread activity has traditionally been associated with woman as weaver and spinster. Thus Rich uses this image to suggest that women must recreate

themselves, using their traditional powers (for example, by valu-
ing female art forms) and perhaps a new power—female
bonding.

When Rich imagines a male listener, the poetic effects are
slightly different. In "A Primary Ground" she addresses a man
who is husband and father: "And this is how you live: a woman,
children / protect you from the abyss." Her tone is scathing:

> It all seems innocent enough, this sin
> of wedlock: you, your wife, your children
> leaning across the unfilled plates
> passing the salt
> down a cloth ironed by a woman
> with aching legs.

In this last image, Rich expresses sympathy for the woman, contempt for the man who allows himself to be shored up this way.
The family is "the primary ground," as the domestic scene is the
microcosm of the larger political institutions in the patriarchy.
The personal, therefore, becomes political in this and every
poem in the volume.

In the final section of "A Primary Ground," Rich perceives the
results of such a marriage as twofold. First there is "Emptiness /
thrust like a batch of letters to the furthest / dark of a drawer."
She emphasizes, however, the more deleterious effect:

> Your wife's twin sister, speechless
> is dying in the house
> you and your wife take turns
> carrying up the trays,
> understanding her case, trying to make her understand.

These lines indict both husband and wife. Together, they im-
prison the "twin sister," an image of the dark, wild side of woman—the side not subservient to man, the side that is in exile. She
is an echo of Charlotte Brontë's madwoman in the attic, only this
woman is "speechless." Rich's emphasis upon this quality of the
"twin sister" is characteristic of certain themes and interests
throughout her poetry. She herself once found that "the unsaid

word" was "the hardest thing to learn." Since her first volume of poetry she has unlearned it. All around her, however, she sees women "speechless" about the kinds of situations depicted in "A Primary Ground."

Whether she addresses a man, as in "A Primary Ground," or a woman, as in "When We Dead Awaken," Rich continues to explore the concept that the personal is the political. It is her unifying vision. Her tone is, however, quite different in the two poems. In "When We Dead Awaken" she addresses the woman in a sympathetic manner and finds likenesses with herself. There is no sympathy for the man in "A Primary Ground." He is the oppressor, benevolent but deadly to the total, human functioning of the woman. He is beyond hope and there is no joint activity that he and the speaker can engage in. His power is predicated upon the submission of his wife, imaged as the continued imprisonment of her "twin sister." Rich's persona would do everything in her power to transform that woman's silence into speech.

The poetic energy of Rich's poems addressing a female audience can be located, therefore, in the dialectic between Rich's female speaker and her more silent sister. The poem that makes this dialectic most apparent is "The Mirror in Which Two Are Seen as one," written in three parts. The first two sections are about love: a woman's love for her "sister" and "Romantic" love as that which enervates women ("love-apples cramp you sideways / with sudden emptiness").

Although the speaker of the poem avoids the use of the first-person pronoun, the "you" functions here as an "I" who supposes that others share her vision: "She is the one *you* call sister." Rich uses this device to link her speaker with other women, just as the mirror of the title suggests that the two women in the poem are reflections of one perceiver. In dialectical terms, they become thesis and antithesis. Thus the true speaker of the poem is not the "you," but she who reconciles the two women. The poem is that process of reconciliation.

The two women in the poem are quite different, opposite in

fact. The "you" is more knowledgeable and characterized by a frenetic energy. Her dynamic quality is conveyed in images associated with fire:

> You blaze like lightning about the room
> flicker around her like fire
> dazzle yourself in her wide eyes
> listing her unfelt needs
> thrusting the tenets of your life
> into her hands.

She would like the other woman to catch some of her fire, an appropriate metaphor for the creative power that the other woman has denied herself. Not at all hesitant, she articulates the "unfelt needs" of her sister. Again, the element of superior intelligence enters; in addition, *thrusting* suggests her aggressiveness. Altogether, such associations carry masculine overtones.

In contrast to the "you's" aggressiveness, the traditional femininity of the sister stands out:

> She moves through a world of India print
> her body dappled
> with softness, the paisley swells at her hip
> walking the street in her cotton shift
> buying fresh figs because you love them
> photographing the ghetto because you took her there

She is drawn in words that suggest her physicality, her "softness," and her desire to please another rather than herself. In this instance, that "other" happens to be a woman. The dialectic between these two women with two different styles results in a synthesis. Both of them change slightly:

> Why are you crying dry up your tears
> we are sisters
> words fail you in the stare of her hunger
> you hand her another book
> scored by your pencil
> you hand her a record
> of two flutes in India reciting

The "you" becomes softer in her caring and she tries to comfort: "Why are you crying." She becomes less frenzied and less dependent on her words and her superior intellect. Even so, there is "another book / scored by your pencil," signifying an ongoing attempt to influence the other by intellectual means. Not all intellectual, she makes a gift of "a record / of two flutes in India reciting." This last image pulls together the two strands of the dialectic: it is an image of harmony that partakes of elements of both women. First, it is Indian music and recalls the sister's dress in "India print." Thus her nature is recognized. Secondly, the verb *reciting* with its connotations of speech recognizes the more aggressive woman's need to articulate, to put into words those "unfelt needs." Finally, the first-person plural pronoun is used for the first time in "we are sisters." Appropriately, this phrase signifies the coming together of the two opposites. Thus the dialectical synthesis patterns the love theme of the poem.

In the last section a universal love for "women who died in childbirth" generates a dream in which the speaker becomes a midwife to herself and other women:

> Dreams of your sister's birth
> your mother dying in childbirth over and over
> not knowing how to stop
> bearing you over and over
>
> your mother dead and you unborn
> your two hands grasping your head
> drawing it down against the blade of life
> your nerves the nerves of a midwife
> learning her trade

Certainly this image is female in its overwhelming emphasis on the process of giving birth. As a midwife would assist a woman in childbirth, so too would the speaker become her own midwife: "Your two hands grasping your head / drawing it down." This birth, however, requires no participation of man. Sexless in the traditional sense of intercourse with another, it is violent (the "head" drawn "against the blade of life") and businesslike (a "trade"). As a deliberate, conscious act, it defies the stereotypes of female passivity and submission and transforms the female ability to endure pain into something profoundly spiritual.

Neither the experience nor the institution of motherhood has accorded many women the birth of self recounted in "The Mirror." On the contrary, as Rich writes in *Of Woman Born*, "the self-denying, self-annihilative role of the Good Mother (linked implicitly with suffering and with the repression of anger) will spell the 'death' of the woman or girl who once had hopes, expectations, fantasies for herself—especially when those hopes and fantasies have never been acted-on." In addition, she points out that "pregnancy may be experienced as the extinguishing of an earlier self," not necessarily to the advantage of the woman's own growth (p. 161).

With its emphasis upon conscious control ("grasping," "drawing it down," and "learning her trade"), the last image of "The Mirror" obviates the mindless, passive birthing of the woman who dies "in childbirth over and over / not knowing how to stop." Furthermore, Adrienne Rich can imagine "women who died at birth" achieving a rebirth that will transform traditional notions of what it means to be a woman. There is a new, raw power in the "nerves of a midwife / learning her trade." The forcefulness of this image manifests the power-to-control trying to become the power-to-transform. Rich assumes that women are transformable. In most respects, the dead who awaken in *Diving into the Wreck* are female, not male. A brief look at a poem addressing a man will clarify this point and its significance in relationship to Rich's developing female aesthetic.

"From a Survivor" works as a monologue in which the speaker, the "survivor," addresses someone who is dead. From the beginning of the poem we learn that the persons involved are a man and a woman and that the subject, at least in the beginning, is their marriage: "The pact that we made was the ordinary pact / of men and women in those days." In the last section of the poem, she mentions that "Next year it would have been 20 years"—for Adrienne Rich, her twentieth wedding anniversary. Tragically,

her husband committed suicide—"and you are wastefully dead."
The speaker is the poet as widow. Consonant with the dominant
motif of the book (the wreck), the survivor speaks of "the failures
of the race" and how she and her husband shared in them, con-
ceivably because their marriage failed. Her tone is poignant as she
recalls her husband:

> Your body is as vivid to me
> as it ever was: even more
>
> since my feeling for it is clearer:
> I know what it could do and could not do
>
> It is no longer
> the body of a god
> or anything with power over my life

Nor over his life. The key difference between this poem with its
imagined male listener and a poem like "The Mirror" is that
Adrienne Rich cannot imagine a rebirth for a man. Her audience
in "From a Survivor" is a dead man who remains dead; in contrast, the widow is energized. She makes "the leap / we talked,
too late, of making." Although she expresses her regret that he is
no longer with her ("wastefully dead"), the widow's ability to
change and grow comes from the removal of her husband's
power over her life. Rich's aesthetic values the separation of
woman from the power of man. She speaks of the leap:

> which I live now
> not as a leap
> but as a succession of brief, amazing movements
>
> each one making possible the next

In this passage, Adrienne Rich defines the power-to-transform.
Granted that Rich's conversational tone in this poem makes
metaphor inappropriate. Even so, she does not attempt to par-
ticularize these "movements," talking *about* them instead of *into*
them. Abstractions ("succession," "movements," "the next") by
their very nature do not possess the liveliness or connecting ability of metaphor. In her poems addressed to a female audience,
Rich handles the notion of transforming power with more im-

mediacy—that is, the best landscape for Rich's imagination is a place where she speaks not to men, whom she considers moribund, but to and for other women and herself. We find this landscape in "Waking in the Dark," "Incipience," "The Mirror," "Song," and most of the other poems in *Diving into the Wreck*. For Rich, only women possess the necessary spark of life that leads to transformation and makes art possible.

When the poet imagines a mixed audience and when she herself assumes an androgynous mask, as in "Diving into the Wreck," the effects are different again. The androgynous ideal is a transitional stage in the formulation of Adrienne Rich's developing aesthetic of female power. Men have botched things; female models of energizing, transforming power are precious and few—for example, Caroline Herschel in "Planetarium." It makes sense to think of balancing the masculine power-to-control with the coming into consciousness of the female power-to-transform. "Diving into the Wreck" is such a poem. In it, the two kinds of power merge.

"Diving into the Wreck" is a narrative poem that becomes an allegory of a modern hero. Rich adopts as her motif the actions of a fully equipped scuba diver who goes alone, "not like Cousteau with his / assiduous team," to explore a sunken ship that may hold precious cargo. We could assume that Rich's persona is female since most of her speakers are women, but Rich's handling of the speaker-diver defies any easy sexual categorization. At first, Rich describes the diver's careful, even methodical preparations for the dive, emphasizing the extreme consciousness of the diver's activity:

> First having read the book of myths,
> and loaded the camera,
> and checked the edge of the knife-blade,
> I put on
> the body-armor of black rubber
> the absurd flippers
> the grave and awkward mask.

The deliberate, conscious action ("read," "loaded," "checked"), the solitariness of the one involved, and the diving into the depths are all familiar motifs in the archetypal pattern of the journey of the male hero. Beowulf, for example, makes a similar dive into the mere to seek vengeance on Grendel's mother. Like Beowulf, the diver goes down into the water and experiences the power that comes with the heroic venture:

> First the air is blue and then
> it is bluer and then green and then
> black I am blacking out and yet
> my mask is powerful
> it pumps my blood with power

We might conclude at this point that the diver is, if not male, then masculine. Such a reading would make sense of the various points of emphasis, particularly the power of the mask to control the effects of nature. Rich constantly defines masculinity as power-over. Such power gets her diver to the midpoint of the poem. Then the sea, as feminine element, transforms:

> the sea is another story
> the sea is not a question of power
> I have to learn alone
> to turn my body without force
> in the deep element.

The diver must adjust to the sea, but no battle takes place as in the traditional stories of male heroes. Instead there is ease. Rich, in effect, is creating a new kind of myth not predicated on power-over the "terrible mother," but an entering into the eternal feminine as into the womb of a mother—or a sister.

Although the diver says, "it is easy to forget / what I came for," the original intent holds: "I came to explore the wreck." Thus the speaker maintains the same kind of consciousness so evident at the beginning. All that has occurred is a merging of powers. That merging, the union of the masculine and the feminine, becomes the major action of the poem and characterizes its central actor. Neither male nor female, the diver is the androgyne:

> This is the place.
> And I am here, the mermaid whose dark hair

153

> streams black, the merman in his armored body
> We circle silently
> about the wreck
> we dive into the hold.
> I am she: I am he

The explicitness of the opening lines ("This is the place. / And I am here") turns slightly ambiguous because of Rich's concision and her use of punctuation. Perhaps there are three people: the diver, the mermaid, and the merman. Together, all three of them "circle silently." This reading might be possible were it not for the last line, "I am she: I am he." Indeed, there is only one person—the androgyne—a man-woman, woman-man. In the lines, "And I am here, the mermaid . . . / the merman," the male and female creatures must be read as composing the "I."

"Diving into the Wreck" expands at the end of the poem to include more than the speaker in this journey of discovery. Even so, the diver maintains the solitary quality of the psychic adventure:

> We are, I am, you are
> by cowardice or courage
> the one who find our way
> back to this scene.

Rich uses the grammatically awkward "one" to emphasize that each of us must complete the journey alone. As individuals we contain both masculine and feminine. Only in their harmonious balance, this poem asserts, do we attain our full humanity. In androgyny, Rich finds—in the seascape of this poem—the solution to "the failures of the race." Clearly there is a difference between man as the enemy (as in "Rape") and the qualities of intelligence and searching determination that our culture defines as masculine and therefore taboo for women. In her foreword to *On Lies, Secrets, and Silence* (1979), Rich addresses women and demands these qualities: "the impulse to puzzle out, brood upon, look up in the dictionary, mutter over, argue about, turn inside-out in verbal euphoria. . . ." She speaks of the present as "a moment in history when women, the majority of the world's people, have become most aware of our need for real literacy, for our own history, more searchingly aware of the lies and distortions of the culture men have devised, when we are finally prepared to take on the most complex, subtle, and drastic revaluation ever attempted of the condition of the species" (p. 12).

While her aim in this foreword to her selected prose is "to define a female consciousness which is political, aesthetic, and erotic, and which refuses to be included or contained in the culture of passivity" (p. 18), Rich's "Diving into the Wreck" is addressed to all humans and does not assume that only females are capable of rebirth and transformation into androgynes. The diver finds that both male and female are "half-destroyed":

> I am she: I am he
>
> whose drowned face sleeps with open eyes
> whose breasts still bear the stress
> . . . .
> we are the half-destroyed instruments
> that once held to a course

A man who is "half-destroyed" has denied the woman in him; a woman, just the opposite. Both "once held to a course"; both, however, must become whole again so that they can function properly. We are, as in Rich's poem, "instruments." Referring at the close of the poem to the "book of myths" which her diver consulted at the start of the venture, Rich's speaker notes that in it "our names do not appear." If our names do not appear in the myths, they have no reality for us. If we are male-female, female-male, then pure "masculinity" is a myth; femininity likewise. Diving into the wreck, we discover this truth: "the wreck and not the story of the wreck / the thing itself and not the myth." If the wreck constitutes "the failures of the race," then we failed because we allowed the myth of sexual differentiation to control us.

The androgynous ideal as a vision of human wholeness and the health of the race is nothing new. Rich has simply discovered it for herself, as she writes in "The Stranger":

I am the androgyne
I am the living mind you fail to describe
in your dead language
the lost noun, the verb surviving
only in the infinitive
the letters of my name are written under the lids
of the newborn child.

Rich focuses on the connection between language and androgyny. She can find no words to fit her present state of being—not that such a condition is new for there is a "lost noun" which once fit. On the other hand, the androgyne is a "verb surviving / only in the infinitive," presumably the verb "to be." Rich places her hope for wholeness in the future and in "the newborn child."

When Rich writes such poems as "Diving into the Wreck" and "The Stranger," she abandons her quest for a female aesthetic, focusing for a time on the ideal of androgyny. In *The Dream of a Common Language* (1978), she repudiates androgyny and emerges as a radical, lesbian poet. In *Diving into the Wreck,* poems like "Rape" and "August" make it clear that Rich finds little to value in men or masculinity. Nor does she find that men are particularly ready to accommodate the new kind of being that she is forging in her poems. She writes in "August":

His mind is too simple, I cannot go on
sharing his nightmares

My own are becoming clearer, they open
into prehistory

which looks like a village lit with blood
where all the fathers are crying: *My son is mine!*

We do not know what kind of nightmares man is having; possibly they are filled with "women in the shape of monsters." The speaker's own nightmares "are becoming clearer" in that she recognizes the denial of the female that goes back to "prehistory." How can there be a merging of the female with the male if the male has never recognized the value of woman? Rich does not admit any exceptions. With the conclusion of "August" in her mind, we can comprehend Rich's subsequent disclaimer of androgyny in *The Dream of a Common Language,* where in "Natural Resources" she writes:

> There are words I cannot choose again:
> *humanism   androgyny*
>
> Such words have no shame in them, no diffidence
> before the raging stoic grandmothers.

The "grandmothers" could possibly refer to all the women throughout history who have been denied by "the fathers" in their preference for the male over the female. Adrienne Rich's poetry attempts to redress this imbalance with her focus on women, her female imagery, and the drive she has to develop a female aesthetic in poems addressed to women and shaped by this focus on the female, not the male, and not the androgyne, despite the explicit direction of her title poem.

Paradoxically, Rich's advocacy of androgyny in her title poem runs contrary to the thematic impulse of other poems that denigrate masculinity and call for a strong, new, female being. *Diving into the Wreck,* therefore, lacks thematic coherence. This is not bad; it simply points up a disjunction in Rich's sensibility. The title poem is a brilliant allegory of our times, and the "tragedy of sex" is certainly a major theme in contemporary literature. Rich's attempt to connect the personal and the political—Vietnam and the lovers' bed—is grand and risky. In the political sweep of this volume she goes against the mainstream of American poetry, which is seemingly content to explore the egotistical sublime. Because she risks much, her failures are more obvious.

With the passion of the recently converted, she sees everything through the lens of radical feminism. For all but "true believers," there is always more than "one whole," even when the tenets of feminism make a good deal of sense: men can be beasts; women are oppressed. Rich's feminism, however, leads her to dogmatism and to the denigration of half of the species. Her hatred of men may seem nervy at first; afterward it leaves a bad taste, as if she is engaged upon a private vendetta. And she is.

Rich's *Sources* (1982) explores the personal issues that shaped the attitudes we see reflected in *Diving into the Wreck*. Addressing her father, dead for many years, she writes: "After your death I met you again as the face of patriarchy, could name at last precisely the principle you embodied, there was an ideology at last which let me dispose of you, identify the suffering you caused, hate you righteously as part of a system, the kingdom of the fathers."[3] This passage allows us to read the more angry feminist poems of *Diving into the Wreck* as a stage in Rich's development and, in part, a personal vendetta against her domineering father, who "taught [her] to hold reading and writing sacred: the eldest daughter in a house with no son, she who must overthrow the father, take what he taught her and use it against him." Had she recognized this private anger a decade earlier, the poems would have been different—less "righteous," less dogmatic, and less searing.

Complicating Rich's anger toward her father—"the face of patriarchy"—is her husband's suicide, an event that must have left her in a riot of confused feelings. As she says in "The Phenomenology of Anger," "Madness. Suicide. Murder. / Is there no way out but these?" Although Rich chose not to write directly about her husband's death, his suicide and her "sexual wounds" color *Diving into the Wreck*. In *Sources*, she will address him, saying "I've had a sense of protecting your existence, not using it merely as a theme for poetry or tragic musing" (p. 32).

Rich's tact can only earn our respect and help us to regard *Diving into the Wreck* as a very human book indeed. Although her stance is dogmatic, she is as "wounded" and troubled as any of us. She articulates her truth—the need for a womanly power to counter the insanity of the nuclear age—and it allows her to become "the survivor" she is. Clearly, Rich's poetic energy flows toward the life-enhancing direction she sees in women. The poems in *The Dream of a Common Language* advance toward a fuller, richer rendering of her vision.

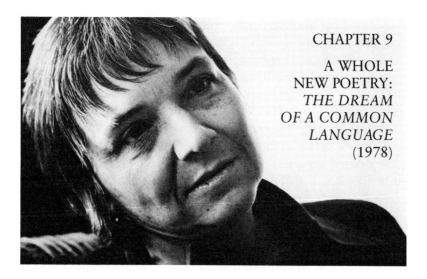

CHAPTER 9

A WHOLE
NEW POETRY:
*THE DREAM
OF A COMMON
LANGUAGE*
(1978)

THE TITLE of Adrienne Rich's *The Dream of a Common Language* recalls Wordsworth's advocacy of a "common" language for poetry in his 1802 preface to the *Lyrical Ballads*. Wordsworth was rebelling against an overly refined poetic diction that limited the audience of poetry along class lines. Although he stresses relationship, as does Rich, Wordsworth's intent was to restore through poetry the integrity and value of emotional life, that which binds us together as human beings below layers of rationality and civilized behavior. While Adrienne Rich certainly has no quarrel with these aims as far as they go, her poetry emphasizes what is "common" among women and her poetic career is a profound rebellion against Wordsworth's dictum that the poet is "a man speaking to men." For Rich, the poet is a woman speaking to other women, and her "dream of a common language" is emblematic of her desire to address that audience.

As she explains elsewhere, "the point . . . is not the 'exclusion' of men; it is that primary presence of women to ourselves and each other . . . which is the crucible of a new language" (*On Lies, Secrets, and Silence*, p. 249). All of these matters are immediately apparent in *The Dream of a Common Language*— poems written by a woman, for and about other women and herself. In the middle of the collection Rich places a group of "Twenty-one Love Poems" written about her relationship with another woman. These love poems plus the overt feminism of the book as a whole heighten the "exclusion" of men, even if that is not the point, and raise the question of the "commonality" of a language restricted to one sex.

In her "dream," Rich is rebelling against man's language and male domination of the world. She asserts a different sort of vision based on what is "common" in and to women. She defines "common" as:

> The interaction of oppression and strength, damage and beauty. It is, quite simply, the *ordinary* in women which will "rise" in every sense of the word—spiritually and in activism. For us to be "extraordinary" or "uncommon" is to fail. History has been embellished with "extraordinary," "exemplary," "uncommon," and of course "token" women whose lives have left the rest unchanged. The "common woman" is in fact the embodiment of the extraordinary will-to-survival in millions of obscure women, a life-force which transcends child-bearing: unquenchable, chromosomatic reality. Only when we can count on this force in each other, everywhere, know absolutely that it is there for us, will we cease abandoning and being abandoned by "all of our lovers." (*On Lies, Secrets, and Silence*, p. 255)

Rich adopts a polemical tone in this passage because her intent is to raise women's consciousness. Thus she names what is most noble and beautiful in the female as that which is *common*. Even kings may suffer, but only an underclass is oppressed. When strength interacts with that oppression, we have what is common in women. Likewise, when beauty remains no matter what damage has been done, then we discover something "unquenchable." When Rich restricts this phenomenal life-force to women, however, her ideology clearly dominates.

There are several reasons why ideology, in particular the feminist cause, has taken over Rich's consciousness in both her prose and poetry. Because she is susceptible to idealism, she responds with fervor to the goals of feminism—a quest for the liberation, both inner and outer, of womankind. She writes in "Sources," her long, meditative poem published in 1983, of herself as:

> The faithful drudging child
> the child at the oak desk whose penmanship,
> hard work, style will win her prizes
> becomes the woman with a mission, not to win prizes
> but to change the laws of history.

Of this same child, she writes, "Say that she grew up in a house / with talk of books, ideal societies. . . ." Feminism, as a vision of an ideal society, becomes Rich's faith. In the same manner, she embraces lesbianism. Her most intimate personal relationship becomes a reflection of her political and social idealism. Thus the life and the work of Adrienne Rich is an integrated whole. At the root of this integration is an ideology that champions the common woman.

Rich, however, is clearly an extraordinary woman with gifts that separate her from the common woman. Her dream or ultimate goal is to use her gifts to forge connections. As the contemporary poet Olga Broumas points out in her review of *The Dream of a Common Language*, "Rich has extraordinary powers—of perception, eloquence, rhythm, courage, the rare fusion of vision and action, the ability to suggest not only to others but to herself a course of action in the mind and follow it in the next breath in the world" (*Reading Adrienne Rich*, pp. 276–77). Every one of Rich's "powers" raises her above the common woman. This would not matter to a less extraordinary woman who lacks Rich's tremendous social conscience and sense of destiny as a poet. Above all, Adrienne Rich does not want to be one of those "token women whose lives have left the rest unchanged."

If we take Rich at her word, she wants to be of use to women. This is the avowed purpose of her volume and a program articulated in her prose. At the same time, Rich's focus on a female audience and subject matter raises the whole issue of literary history and its exclusion of women and women writers. There have been exceptions, of course, but Rich does not want to be one of them. She wants to change the course of poetry itself and have it admit a female aesthetic. For her, such an aesthetic is based upon womanly power. She does not mean "the old patriarchal power-over but the power-to-create, power-to-think, power-to-articulate and concretize our visions and transform our lives and those of our children" (*On Lies, Secrets, and Silence*, p. 271). *The Dream of a Common Language,* therefore, brings her aesthetics of power to its culmination.

At the root of this power is the development of a common language for women that has nothing to do with specific words or sentence patterns, but with language as a system for making connections. For Adrienne Rich, poetry is the vehicle for this common language and her metaphor for it. She believes that "Poetry is above all a concentration of the power of language, which is the power of our ultimate relationship to everything in the universe. It is as if forces we can lay claim to in no other way become present to us in sensuous form" (*On Lies, Secrets, and Silence,* p. 248). For her, "there is nothing more unnerving and yet empowering than the making of connections" (p. 255). Poems, therefore, become a model for connectiveness, demonstrate the capacity for making connections, and put the "dream of a common language" in sensuous form. If the lives of uncommon women "have left the rest unchanged," Rich's "dream"— or vision, in this instance—imagines a different outcome. In sum, Adrienne Rich's poetry in this volume addresses the issues of womanly power and the drive to connect in poetry and in personal relationships.

She undertakes different strategies to forge those connections, sometimes in an impersonal voice, sometimes in her own voice speaking directly about these issues. When she speaks in a voice that is "no longer personal" in the attempt to achieve that common language, she strains for the unattainable. Poetry, at least in our age, depends upon the individual voice. Our poets are condemned to the personal and to the heroic attempt to stretch its bounds. Part of the poignancy of reading *The Dream of a Common Language* lies in observing Rich's aesthetic development as she comes to grips with the limitations of lyrical poetry. Realizing her dream is an unattainable vision, she shapes a new, less grandiose aesthetic.

The development of this new aesthetic begins with "Power," Rich's opening poem about Marie Curie. In this poem, Rich establishes one of the main directions of *The Dream of a Common Language*. She explores the multifaceted issue of women and power, exposing in the first group of poems her obsession with the deaths of women like Marie Curie, Elvira Shatayev, and some women mountain climbers. A "famous woman" like Marie Curie had power, yet her scientific discovery of radium killed her. In effect, Rich sees the danger involved in the kind of power available to an "uncommon" woman. Such power drains the woman and Rich abjures it. By the end of the book, however, Rich moves toward a more positive definition of power and "a whole new poetry." Central to this poetic is a womanly power that involves "no mere will to mastery," as in Marie Curie's endeavors, but "only care for the many-lived unending forms." The way the poet approaches this "new poetry" unfolds in the three-part structure of the volume.

In "Power," Rich begins her study in a poem loosely associative in its parts. The first line announces both theme and metaphor. A fragment broken between its two phrases to indicate a partial stop, "Living   in the earth deposits   of our history" suggests the presentness of the past. The narrator makes a literal discovery of her heritage in a bottle unearthed by a farm machine and then later in a book about Marie Curie.

> Living   in the earth-deposits   of our history
>
> Today a backhoe divulged   out of a crumbling flank of earth
> one bottle   amber   perfect   a hundred-year-old
> cure for fever   or melancholy   a tonic
> for living on this earth   in the winters of this climate
>
> Today I was reading about Marie Curie:
> she must have known she suffered   from radiation sickness
> her body bombarded for years   by the element
> she had purified

It seems she denied to the end
the source of the cataracts on her eyes
the cracked and suppurating skin   of her finger-ends
till she could no longer hold   a test-tube or a pencil

She died   a famous woman   denying
her wounds
denying
her wounds   came   from the same source as her power

No explicit connection is made between the artifact and Marie Curie, except to suggest that neither the tonic in the bottle nor Curie's radium has especially cured humanity's ills. Rich is not interested in Marie Curie's scientific discovery that will ensure her continued fame beyond her death. Instead she is trying to understand the nature of power, specifically womanly power. Rich comes to the enigmatic conclusion that "her wounds   came   from the same source as her power" and that Curie denied this connection. Clearly, making such a connection would be "empowering"; otherwise, her wounds cancel her power. In this manner, Rich denigrates Curie's power because she did not accept the ordinary woman in herself—that "interaction" of "damage and beauty" that is common to womankind.

Just as finding the "cure for fever or melancholy" in her garden makes the speaker wonder about the value of what survives the historical process, so too does reading about Marie Curie leave her feeling dissatisfied with the achievements of extraordinary women. Besides killing Marie Curie, that achievement is truly negative if all it does is enhance the reputation of one woman. Since the poem does not mention other women we can only leave ourselves open to the implications of its abstractions: *wounds* and *power*. It helps to know that Rich has said elsewhere that "For us to be 'extraordinary' or 'uncommon' is to fail." Nonetheless, the poem's abstractions make it less effective than it could be. Rich's subsequent poem, "Phantasia for Elvira Shatayev," however, does provide a counterpoint.

The second poem in the book concerns the actions of a group

of women—a climbing team, all of whom died in a storm on Lenin Peak in August 1974. Seerlike, the voice in the poem comes from Elvira Shatayev, the team leader. She speaks to her husband, imagines his finding and burying the women's bodies, and addresses the issue of mortality. As counterpoint, "Phantasia for Elvira Shatayev" parallels the theme of "Power" but forms a contrast in that the drive to power is communal, not singular as in Marie Curie's case. Even so, the fate of all the women is death. The "Phantasia" of the title is a musical term defined variously around a "free flight of fancy."[1] The most appropriate definition would be "a character piece of the Romantic era" with Shatayev as the character; also a fantasia "indicates a dreamlike mood"—in this poem the vision that emerges from Shatayev's "sleep."

This vision unfolds in three sections, the lines of each clustering around separate aspects of Rich's theme. That is, when women channel their energies into a common effort—climbing the mountain—their action transcends their mortality. We have had tales of the Amazons, but here Rich describes a recent event, transmogrified by an imagined rendering of one woman's consciousness. The first section (lines 1–18) deals with a retrospective of how the women died, although the speaker never admits their death: "the wind / died down and we slept." She focuses upon the group's action in preparing themselves for the climb and she speaks "with a voice no longer personal," followed in parentheses by "I want to say   *with voices*" (Rich's italics). These lines echo Rich's "Meditations for a Savage Child" in *Diving into the Wreck* with one key variation from "a language no longer personal." The import of the variation is twofold. On the one hand, Elvira Shatayev has transcended her own personal, subjective self by joining with the other women on the climbing team. Then, when she corrects herself and says "voices," she avows the communal effort. This solo is truly a chorus. In their bonding together, all the women have risen above their separate selves. Elvira Shatayev just happens to be the persona Rich chooses to translate the women's voices into a song—a "Phantasia." Clearly, it is but one step further to "a language no longer personal," a language the poet is able to give voice to as she centers upon woman's common experience. The efforts of the mountain climbing team provide a remarkable instance.

In the middle of the poem Shatayev imagines her husband climbing the same mountain to find and bury the bodies. Although she recognizes her husband's love for her, she points out the key difference between them: "You climbed here for yourself / we climbed for ourselves." Whereas the man is singular and egocentric, the women share a common goal that empowers them. In her diary Shatayev writes, "*I have never loved / like this   I have never seen / my own forces so taken up and shared / and given back.*" The love the women have for each other is compared with the husband's love for his wife, which appears as selfish as his mountain climbing. The man is clearly limited and incapable of participating in the transcendental endeavor of the women. Shatayev's husband cannot succeed. Even though he makes a monumental effort to bury all the women's bodies, this effort is seen as not good enough. He is not a woman; therefore, he cannot love as a woman can. Seen this way, the poem has its absurd side. Any sort of chauvinism risks absurdity; female chauvinism is no exception. Rich's "impersonal" voice drives her to this extreme.

The "Phantasia" develops a polemical tone in the following passage. Rich has a cause to advance and a man to put behind her:

> When you have buried us   told your story
> ours does not end   we stream
> into the unfinished   the unbegun
> the possible
> Every cell's core of heat   pulsed out of us
> into the thin air   of the universe
> the armature of rock beneath these snows
> this mountain   which has taken   the imprint of our minds
> through changes elemental and minute
> as those we underwent

> to bring each other here
> choosing ourselves   each other   and this life
> whose every breath   and grasp   and further foothold
> is somewhere   still enacted   and continuing

Rich's feminist vision is rendered here in remarkable poetry. Her theme is the transcendence of the women and their immortality. "Program" and poetry cohere as Rich affirms the strength inherent in the action of the women joining in a common effort "to bring each other here." Such female energy is new and potent enough to transcend the limits of space, time, and mortality.

Olga Broumas speaks of Rich's "eloquence, rhythm and courage." The first two qualities clearly appear in the style of the above passage, while courage is the content. Rich's discourse possesses the fluency we demand of eloquence, first because of her diction. The verbs *stream* and *pulsed* establish a metaphorical direction that is then sustained by the syntax. While she abjures punctuation, capitals indicate where a sentence begins. The second sentence, "Every cell's core of heat . . . ," builds in an incremental fashion, each phrase or clause flowing smoothly into the next. The rhythm of these lines can be seen in the regular patterning of a series of triads: "the unfinished the unbegun / the possible." It seems as if Rich is driven to complete her phrases in a series of three items: "choosing ourselves each other and this life." In the last two lines, the triad of "every breath and grasp and further foothold" is reinforced in the rhythmic breaks that make a triad of the last line. This triadic rhythm appears obsessive.

Rich's eloquence in "Phantasia for Elvira Shatayev" is strengthened by a feminist vision that finds its correlative in the experience of the women mountain climbers. The purpose of the poem is to inspire. The self behind the inspirational vision of the "Phantasia" is presented in Rich's third poem, "Origins and History of Consciousness," in which Rich explores the personal anguish of her life, particularly her choice to love again. That decision is at the root of her aesthetic as well, for love and poetry have at their root a similar impulse: "The drive to connect." The first part of this long, three-sectioned poem shows us the process by which the poet reaches her insight about poetry and love:

> Night-life. Letters, journals, bourbon
> sloshed in the glass. Poems crucified on the wall,
> dissected, their bird-wings severed
> like trophies. No one lives in this room
> without living through some kind of crisis.
>
> No one lives in this room
> without confronting the whiteness of the wall
> behind the poems, planks of books,
> photographs of dead heroines.
> Without contemplating last and late
> the true nature of poetry. The drive
> to connect. The dream of a common language.
>
> Thinking of lovers, their blind faith, their
> experienced crucifixions,
> my envy is not simple.

The poem opens in a series of fragments, presents an image of "poems crucified" and "dissected," and speaks of the anguish involved in moving from the randomness of everyday life to the creative act itself. The "photographs of dead heroines" are significant because they connect with the two preceding poems and with women like Marie Curie and Elvira Shatayev. At the end of the second stanza, the climactic phrases offset the dismemberment in the syntax and imagery that precede them.

With "the true nature of poetry," the private and particular world of the poet shifts to the universal and abstract. Rich, however, has prepared for this leap with a series of parallel clauses and phrases. At first, these seem predictable: "No one lives in this room / without living through some kind of crisis." Through repetition and variation, a key device of musical composition, Rich generates more tension: "no one lives in this room / without confronting the whiteness of the wall." This clause suggests the blankness or emptiness before the creative act takes over. Or as Rich's title indicates, the "origins of consciousness." Dropping her initial phrase, the poet uses a shortened parallelism: "Without contemplating . . . the true nature of poetry." Poetry has been at least a partial subject for this poem, yet this phrase comes as a semantic surprise. One would expect it of Shelley or Wordsworth, but not of a twentieth-century American woman poet. Rich articulates her definition of poetry and it emerges within the context of everyday life: the poet in *her* study. "The drive to connect" characterizes Rich's consciousness in this book and manifests itself in poems dominated by her feminist vision as well as in the "Twenty-One Love Poems" at the center of the collection.

In Rich's "dream of a common language," poetry commingles with love and speaks of her drive to harmony, generativity, and ideal form. The love of women for one another is more "generative" for Adrienne Rich than heterosexual love because it leads her to a new language. Her vision encompasses an ideal order of society based on the value of woman, not as aberrant and "other" from man, but in the fullness of her powers. An ideal society would be predicated on women "holding back nothing / because we were women"—on bringing "our full power / to every subject," as she says in "Paula Becker to Clara Westhoff," also in this volume.

Bringing the fullness of her powers to these love poems, Rich achieves a remarkable series reminiscent of Shakespeare's sonnets. In a review of *The Dream of a Common Language*, Hayden Carruth goes so far as to call them "true sonnets. For if they do not conform to the prescribed rules, they certainly come from the same lyrical conception that made the sonnet in the first place." Carruth quotes poem 11 in the sequence and then provides an encomium to Rich's achievement:

> It is an outstanding poem but typical as well of Rich's way of writing: the genuinely literate sentences woven into genuinely poetic measures, cadences, and patterns of sound; the easy, perfectly assimilated classical allusion; the sense of immediate, unique experience; the details . . . turned into generalized insights of humane value. These are the resonances which we find in all the poems. A mind is here, a loving mind, in and of this world, including all this world's cultural inheritance, yet still asserting,

firmly and calmly, its own independence and newness. (*Reading
Adrienne Rich*, p. 272)

Of course, the independence and newness that Rich asserts is her
sexual preference and its open proclamation. The "Love Poems"
are extraordinary not simply because they declare one woman's
love for another woman, but because they transcend sex. The
poems are not narrowed by the focus on lesbian love but ex-
panded. By abjuring her willful quest for "a voice no longer
personal" and dealing with extremely personal subject matter
and her own voice, Adrienne Rich paradoxically achieves what
Carruth terms "generalized insight of humane value."

Granted, some of the poems tie their significance tightly to a
strictly female imagery. Poem 6, for example, speaks of the beloved's "small hands, precisely equal to my own." The speaker
says that "in these hands / I could trust the world, or in many
hands like these." The poem asserts Rich's preference for women
in positions of power and extends her vision of women's capabilities. In poem 12 she speaks of "two lovers of one gender
/ . . . two women of one generation." And in the "Floating
Poem, Unnumbered," the subject is the lovemaking between two
women: "Your traveled, generous thighs / between which my
whole face has come and come." Despite the specific focus and
explicitness of poems such as these, the majority of the love
poems achieve a universal significance.

Poem 3, for example, describes the emotional climate at the
beginning of the love relationship. When one is middle-aged,
falling in love contains a quality of excitement and joy unavail-
able to the young. As the poem moves toward its conclusion, the
tone modulates:

> Since we're not young, weeks have to do time
> for years of missing each other. Yet only this odd warp
> in time tells me we're not young.
> Did I ever walk the morning streets at twenty,
> my limbs streaming with a purer joy?
> did I lean from any window over the city
> listening for the future
> as I listen here with nerves tuned for your ring?

And you, you move toward me with the same tempo.
Your eyes are everlasting, the green spark
of the blue-eyed grass of early summer,
the green-blue wild cress washed by the spring.
At twenty, yes: we thought we'd live forever.
At forty-five, I want to know even our limits.
I touch you knowing we weren't born tomorrow,
and somehow, each of us will help the other live,
and somewhere, each of us must help the other die.

No longer young, the lovers must make up for time lost when they were not loving each other. They must not waste time because they do not possess the luxury of unspent decades. Yet this is not a lover's complaint, but a paean to love at forty-five, a reciprocated love that gives birth to the image of the beloved's eyes, which are "everlasting." The speaker notes the color of these eyes and their kinship with the "green spark / of the blue-green grass of early summer." This image defies age or aging, yet the speaker insists on loving without illusions. She wants "to know even our limits." The poem concludes on a note of somber tenderness in a voice eminently mature. She is not so transported by the joy of love and the contemplation of the beloved that she loses sight of their finiteness. She imagines that finiteness shared, which tempers the solemnity of the last line: "and somewhere, each of us must help the other die."

A comparison with Shakespearean sonnets and this one by Adrienne Rich need not be glib. Both set the praise of the beloved within the context of time passing. Both mix realism with idealism. In each, the felicity of phrase makes for memorable lines. In this comparison, Rich suffers in terms of quantity, but her themes are as sonorous and as deeply felt. While the reviewer Olga Broumas does not mention Shakespeare, she does find the "Twenty-One Love Poems" striking and states that "The gesture of these poems is one of desire for a totality of living, openness, communication and trust, in the new, the immediate, the real" (*Reading Adrienne Rich*, p. 280). She goes on to cite the first and nineteenth in the sequence and mentions her own expectations for "twenty-one poems about love" and what she found: "one long poem, in twenty-one sections, about a deep and anguished proximity of two lives" (p. 280). No one can read these poems without sensing that "anguish," for these poems speak of the difficulties of a loving relationship and of the "work / heroic in its ordinariness" of "two people together" (poem 19). These poems also speak of the collapse of the "dream of a common language" and a heightened awareness of solitude: the poet's essential, indeed primal, aloneness in the universe.

To illustrate some of these issues, the last poem in the series offers an appropriate and beautiful starting point. In this poem, lines 1–5 establish the setting, a place like Stonehenge, rendered in vivid images with one reference ("a cleft of light") to a previous poem. Lines 6–10 interpret the setting as a mind-set; and lines 11–15 place the speaker within the setting and articulate the theme: "I choose to be . . . a woman." And, she implies, an artist: "to draw this circle."

> The dark lintels, the blue and foreign stones
> of the great round rippled by stone implements
> the midsummer night light rising from beneath
> the horizon—when I said "a cleft of light"
> I meant this. And this is not Stonehenge
> simply nor any place but the mind
> casting back to where her solitude,
> shared, could be chosen without loneliness,
> not easily nor without pains to stake out
> the circle, the heavy shadows, the great light.
> I choose to be a figure in that light,
> half-blotted by darkness, something moving
> across that space, the color of stone
> greeting the moon, yet more than stone:
> a woman. I choose to walk here. And to draw this circle.

It is difficult to see this poem as a love poem. We search for the beloved and find only an oblique reference to "solitude, / shared, . . . chosen without loneliness." The love in this poem is for womanliness and can be seen in the choice of setting, the time of year, and the image of the moon. The speaker's mind finds an image of itself in Stonehenge, an ancient site in England whose purpose remains shrouded despite much scientific analysis and speculation. What matters here is that the speaker responds to its spiritual resonances and its connection to the moon. It is a woman's place in its shape—a "great round" suggestive of the womb. At midsummer, even to this day, rituals are held at such places to celebrate the harvest, the bounty given by Mother Earth. The moon, a female image, just as the sun is an image of male power and light, is "the midsummer nightlight." The speaker's point is that it has taken her a great deal, "not easily nor without pain" to reach this place. That is, she becomes aware of the utter centrality of her womanliness and her connection to an ancient, prehistoric sense of the earth as the female principle and of herself as "something moving / across that space . . . / a woman." Rich stresses the role of her consciousness when she emphasizes: "I *choose* to walk here. And to draw this circle." In coming to love the womanliness of her mind and its images, she comes to love herself. This love is not solipsistic, but radiant. It glows in "a cleft of light."

For the thematic significance of *light* we have to go back to love poem 18, where Rich first uses the phrase "a cleft of light." In her first reference she is unsure what she means by it, but it appears in a context where Rich experiences her aloneness even from the beloved woman:

> I feel estrangement, yes. As I've felt dawn
> pushing toward daybreak. Something: a cleft of light—?
> Close between grief and anger, a space opens
> where I am Adrienne alone. And growing colder.

We could read the estrangement as something positive that leads toward the light, or greater understanding. It is "dawn / pushing toward daybreak." Estrangement thus becomes merely the parting between night and day. Traditionally, this is a life-affirming, optimistic image pattern, except in an aubade, where in the morning a lover has to part from the beloved. In this context, sunrise is regarded as cruel, lovers preferring the dark. The dawn's coming implies, therefore, a separation, a "cleft of light." The speaker is not warmed by the sun, but is "colder." At the end, a more serious theme emerges. The end of the love affair occupies the speaker and makes her aware of her essential aloneness. A "cleft of light" is, then, the finale of "the drive to connect" and the "dream" collapses.

Poem 21 takes the "cleft of light" image and transforms it to something beautiful, primitive, and mystical—a space like Stonehenge. In this space, Rich's persona assumes the role of high priestess. She seeks out "that light" and performs her rituals "to stake out / the circle, the heavy shadows, the great light." Indeed the structure of the image is reminiscent of "Planetarium," where the speaker does not stand in light but is instead "bombarded" by pulsations from the universe. She is "an instrument in the shape of a woman" trying to "translate" those pulsations. In effect, she is a poet. Love poem 21 exhibits an even stronger affirmation of the commitment to poetry, for the speaker "*chooses* to walk here. And to draw this circle." She may part from her beloved, but her connection to the universe and to womanliness is forged by her commitment to the spirit of poetry, which is "the drive to connect."

Rich's technique, as a whole, puts the detail outside of herself first ("the dark lintels, the blue and foreign stones") and then, through her syntax, makes the point that this place is not outside her, but within her. She employs the "not-nor" combination, proceeding toward greater clarity ("not Stonehenge / simply nor any place but the mind"). Thus polarities are resolved, harmony created.

This harmony is significantly different from the tonal qualities of the poems preceding the love poems. In part 1 Rich condescends toward Marie Curie and denigrates her power as an extraordinary woman. In taking on the "voice no longer personal" of Elvira Shatayev, she tries to escape from the trappings of her own mortal condition and to seize transcendence by an act of willful depersonalization. Testing her commitment to "the drive to connect," the love poems also serve to center her once again in the joy and pain of her own experience. While these poems are suffused deeply in womanliness and womanly love, Rich speaks to the human condition and the truths of the heart. We also note small but significant gestures to include the other sex. In poem 19, for example, she writes:

> If I could let you know—
> two women together is a work
> nothing in civilization has made simple,
> two people together is a work
> heroic in its ordinariness,
> the slow-picked, halting traverse of a pitch
> where the fiercest attention becomes routine
> —look at the faces of those who have chosen it.

Those "two people together" are not delineated by sex. Those faces could be female or male; Rich does not specify. In the third part of the volume, this opening up becomes more generous. While Rich does not necessarily include men in her considerations, she does relax her obsessiveness toward female separation.

Entitled "Not Somewhere Else, But Here," the third section of *The Dream of a Common Language* contains poems about and for women. These include: "Paula Becker to Clara Westhoff," "Sibling Mysteries" (dedicated to Rich's sister), the elegiac "A Woman Dead in Her Forties," "Mother-Right," "Natural Resources," and "Transcendental Etude," a poem that articulates the womanly aesthetic the poet has been developing throughout her work. This poem illuminates the kind of power Rich's poetic consciousness embraces in her journey away from the destructive power accorded an uncommon woman in her opening poem.

The final section of "Transcendental Etude" presents Rich's new aesthetic, for there is less *drive* in this poetry, more accomplishment and ease.

> a whole new poetry beginning here.
>
> Vision begins to happen in such a life
> as if a woman quietly walked away
> from the argument and jargon in a room
> and sitting down in the kitchen, began turning in her lap
> bits of yarn, calico and velvet scraps,

laying them out absently on the scrubbed boards
in the lamplight, with small rainbow-colored shells
sent in cotton-wool from somewhere far away,
and skeins of milkweed from the nearest meadow—
original domestic silk, the finest findings—
and the darkblue petal of the petunia,
and the dry darkbrown lace of seaweed;
not forgotten either, the shed silver
whisker of the cat,
the spiral of paper-wasp-nest curling
beside the finch's yellow feather.
Such a composition has nothing to do with eternity,
the striving for greatness, brilliance—
only with the musing of a mind
one with her body, experienced fingers quietly pushing
dark against bright, silk against roughness,
pulling the tenets of a life together
with no mere will to mastery,
only care for the many-lived, unending
forms in which she finds herself,
becoming now the sherd of broken glass
slicing light in a corner, dangerous
to flesh, now the plentiful, soft leaf
that wrapped round the throbbing finger, soothes the wound;
and now the stone foundation, rockshelf further
forming underneath everything that grows.

Rich's active, conscious embracing of woman's art distinguishes
this poem from poems of her early career, particularly those in
which a woman artist is the persona. "Mathilde in Normandy,"
for example, appears in Rich's first book and presents a woman
(Queen Mathilde) working with other women to weave a tapestry. The poem does not emphasize the communal quality of the
women's art. Instead, it centers upon Mathilde's work as a desperate attempt to fill her time while her lord, William the Conqueror, invades a foreign coast. The speaker's tone condescends
toward this "pastime . . . esteemed proper" for ladies. In "Transcendental Etude" Rich does not look down upon the homely,
craftlike quality of woman's art, but articulates the significance

of such work for herself and, by implication, others. Through her diction and imagery, Rich makes clear that her "composition" is not the power-over but the power-to-create with ordinary materials and with natural objects: shells, milkweed, cat's whiskers. These objects are not exclusive, expensive, nor manufactured. They are common, yet not usually found together, thereby exotic and beautiful when placed in the collage composition. Thus they are appropriate to Rich's woman-based aesthetic. Furthermore, separating herself from "the argument and jargon in a room," Rich's persona works in a kitchen, a woman's traditional place. She does not work consciously, but "absently,"—naturally and easily, the way she would approach any common female activity. Thus a feeling of acceptance emerges.

In the middle of the poem, a list of materials dominates. In this piling up of objects, Rich seems more intent on naming than on connecting or envisioning. As she names the materials of her composition, she naturally employs nouns and with them many adjectives. Her parallels and repetitions are simple compounds: "from somewhere far away" and "from the nearest meadow"; "lace of seaweed" and "whisker of the cat." Numerous adjectives loosen the syntax. The process of naming takes over, and with it nouns and adjectives dominate. Gertrude Stein's study of poetry and grammar, though quirky, provides a helpful gloss on this aspect of Rich's newfound poetry, which is, of course, not "new" at all. In Stein's view: "Poetry is concerned with using with abusing, with losing with wanting, with denying with avoiding with adoring with replacing the noun. It is doing that always doing that, doing that and doing nothing but that. Poetry is doing nothing but using losing refusing and pleasing and betraying and caressing nouns."[2] Stein emphasizes the emotional state that arises from such naming with nouns: "Nouns are the name of anything. Think of all that early poetry, think of Homer, think of Chaucer, think of the Bible, and you will see what I mean you will really realize that they were drunk with nouns, to name to know how to name earth sea and sky and all that was in them was enough to make them live and love in names, and that is what poetry is it is a state of knowing and feeling a name."[3]

Thus Adrienne Rich names for us the textures of things that she knows and feels, emphasizing by her list the natural found-object. No purchase is involved in the skeins of milkweed or the petals of petunia—except the purchase of attention to the loveliness of that which cannot be bought and the care involved in seeing individual beauty enhanced by juxtaposition.

Modest, the poetic consciousness in this poem does not strive for "eternity, greatness, brilliance." She does not assume to know it all, just to know well the "many-lived unending / forms in which she finds herself." Breaking through the modesty, the last image proclaims a consciousness that sees itself as the mother of us all, "the stone foundation, rockshelf further / forming underneath everything that grows." If we are reminded of Wordsworth's definition of the poet as "the rock of defense of human nature; an upholder and preserver, carrying everywhere with him relationship and love," the comparison is apt. Change the pronouns and Adrienne Rich fits the concept of the poet as a presence that exists not for itself alone but as an expression of a common consciousness and a common life.

Thus the *drive* to connect is deemphasized. She is not driven; she "quietly walked away." The consciousness in this poem exerts "no mere will to mastery"—"only care." As she muses and quietly pulls "the tenets of a life together," she appears more comfortable with change than she has in previous volumes. She cannot control flux, only be aware of it as she feels its workings within herself. With this loving self-acceptance she achieves the inclusiveness of the last image. Into this vision of being—"the stone foundation . . . forming underneath everything that grows"—anyone could enter. This is not the poetry of an ideologue, but that of one who has absorbed feminism into her being. Thus she becomes more relaxed, infinitely generous. While Rich may not use the term "humanism" anymore, it applies to the posture she takes in "Transcendental Etude."

The "new kind of poetry beginning here" has emerged from Adrienne Rich's commitment to women. This poetry opts for a female audience, for poems about women, and for a common language, one that will connect women and lead women to release the kind of female energy—Mary Daly calls it "gynergy"— that has not been known in the modern world.[4] Adrienne Rich wants to convert the world through women's power-to-transform. *Transform* means to change the nature, function, or condition of—to *convert*. Whether she accomplishes this remains to be seen. More to the point, she articulates her dream as a conscious goal. Thus she earns the label of visionary poet.

As visionary, Adrienne Rich has an awareness of the whole that transcends time and space. As poet, she can both articulate her vision and urge others toward its realization. In *The Dream of a Common Language,* she brings a woman-centered world into focus, as her poem "Natural Resources" makes most evident. In this world, women would reject the role of "other" for man and become subject with all the suffering, pride, and responsibility that goes with such a change in status. Furthermore, it would be a world that values woman's natural resources, including her sense of protection toward life. Section 3 of "Natural Resources" describes how "the routine of life goes on" by means of woman's care and attention:

> a woman turns a doorknob, but so slowly
> so quietly, that no one wakes
>
> and it is she alone who gazes
> into the dark of bedrooms, ascertains
>
> how they sleep, who needs her touch
> what window blows the ice of February
>
> into the room and who must be protected:
> It is only she who sees; who was trained to see.

Although we might object to the female chauvinism reflected here, Rich's vision of the common woman is posed against those forces that throughout history have been directed against the female presence she describes so lovingly.

Rich embraces her own womanhood as well, choosing to be a woman and "to draw this circle," as she writes in love poem 21. Her art is based on her being as a woman. Through poetry she has affected a tremendous change in her own consciousness; her power as a poet is such that she can affect the consciousness of others as well—if they dare to listen. She writes that "the necessity of poetry has to be stated over and over, but only to those who have reason to fear its power, or those who still believe that language is 'only words' and that an old language is good enough for our descriptions of the world we are trying to transform" (*On Lies, Secrets, and Silence,* p. 247).

For Rich, language is not "only words" but connecting power. In the style of her poems, she models this power—that is, she makes bridges across the boundaries that separate words, things, and women from one another. Significantly, however, in the final poem of *The Dream of a Common Language,* the drive to connect no longer dominates. This change confirms that Adrienne Rich has connected her art to her womanhood (in a way different from connecting to the female principle of the *Leaflets* poems). Thus the drive no longer exists. At the same time, she also connects with one of the traditional art forms of women through her use of the quiltlike composition. Most important, she embraces the various aspects of her many-lived self, concluding her book with a magnificent image of human wholeness.

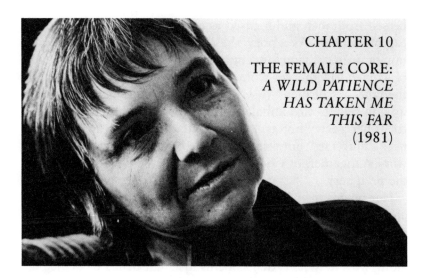

CHAPTER 10

THE FEMALE CORE:
*A WILD PATIENCE
HAS TAKEN ME
THIS FAR*
(1981)

IN *A Wild Patience Has Taken Me This Far,* the power of poetry often seems at war with the power of Adrienne Rich's beliefs, both political and personal. In a key statement about the relationship between poetry and power, Rich defines poetry as "above all a concentration of the *power* of language, which is the power of our ultimate relationship to everything in the universe. It is as if forces we can lay claim to in no other way, become present to us in sensuous form" (*On Lies, Secrets, and Silence,* p. 248). Rich's concept is striking: through poetry that concentrates "the power of language," we can connect with "everything in the universe." In the present volume, however, Rich's beliefs often take precedence over her commitment to the power of poetry.

Since *Diving into the Wreck* (1972) she has thrown her lot with women and embraced feminism. Opting for a community of women and for a womanly power capable of changing the world, she defines herself as a lesbian in *The Dream of a Common Language* (1978) and as a lesbian separatist in the present volume. Whereas *Leaflets* (1969) saw her emergence as a political poet, these later books chart the specific development of her radical feminism. As a lesbian separatist, she has "separated" herself from men and focused as exclusively and lovingly as she can on women. As a poet, she is reacting against "the deprivation of women living for centuries without a poetry which spoke of women together, of women alone, of women as anything but the fantasies of men" (*On Lies, Secrets, and Silence,* pp. 248–49). To redress this imbalance, she approaches the subject matter of her poetry not as "the ultimate relationship to everything in the universe," but selectively. She believes she must write "of women together, of women alone," of a world where man is on the periphery.

Her poems in *A Wild Patience* explore the problem of poetry and belief. "Good" beliefs, be they patriotism, fundamentalism, or lesbian separatism, do not necessarily sweep into their purview good poetry. If the poetry is "good," the belief gets carried along with it. When Rich's poems lose that delicate balance between poetry and belief, they fail. As Louis Zukofsky writes, "If read properly, good poetry does not argue its attitudes or beliefs; it exists independently of the reader's preferences for one kind of 'subject' or another. Its conviction is in its mastery of technique."[1] Whether or not we prefer the lesbian sensibility or Rich's program for poetry, when she convinces us through her "mastery of technique," we find good poems.

The technique that works most successfully in *A Wild Patience* reflects a "post-modernist mode" which Jonathan Holden locates in American poetry of the late 1970s.

> Less and less are poems offered as personal testimony whose prime test is sincerity and authenticity. Although such a contract, after the stultifying impersonality of late-modernism, once seemed to be a breath of fresh air, now it is seen to place too heavy a demand on a poet to scour his own experiences for authentic "material." Recoiling from the demands of testimony, yet still committed to poetry that treats of the self, a poet may now find himself resorting to forms that resemble extended hypotheses instead of testimony, poems that invite the reader to "suppose" and that then proceed to spin a mythology.[2]

When Rich's poems succeed in *A Wild Patience,* they often take the form of "extended hypotheses" rather than of "personal tes-

timony." Since a hypothesis is a supposition, it lends itself naturally to the free play of the imagination. When that freedom is
restricted—as it can be in personal testimony that must seem
authentic and sincere, even artless—the poems fail. Effective
poems could emerge from "personal testimony," for example,
the sequence of love poems in Rich's *The Dream of a Common
Language*. In *A Wild Patience,* however, she "recoils" from the
confessional "demands" of such testimony, as many of her
poems deal with her ongoing relationship with another woman.
When protecting that relationship becomes more important
than the poem itself, the poetry suffers. Her protectiveness also
seems an offshoot of her belief system, that is, her lesbian separatism. The successful poems in *A Wild Patience,* those in which
Rich convinces us by her "mastery of technique," make us less
tolerant of those poems in which her beliefs obtrude, where she
is "protecting" a personal relationship, or where she does not
employ the post-modernist mode.

"Integrity" is one of the most beautiful and convincing poems
in the volume. Its rhythms remind us of the remarkable "Transcendental Etude" in *The Dream of a Common Language,* and
its mythic dimension sets a standard for the poems ranged with
it. Rich herself must have felt that this poem captured the essence of her book, for she selected its first line as her title. The
poem adopts a journey motif, the first part of which takes place
by boat. The journey is hypothetical and presented by the poet
as such:

> A wild patience has taken me this far
>
> as if I had to bring to shore
> a boat with a spasmodic outboard motor
> old sweaters, nets, spray-mottled books
> tossed in the prow
> some kind of sun burning my shoulder-blades.
> Splashing the oarlocks. Burning through.
> Your fore-arms can get scalded, licked with pain
> in a sun blotted like unspoken anger
> behind a casual mist.

Once she has caught our attention with her striking first line, Rich enters the hypothetical situation with the simple phrase *as if.* She invites us to *suppose* with her—that she has had a certain responsibility—not to set forth on an adventure, but "to bring to shore / a boat." This task involves difficulties because the basic equipment is not terribly reliable ("a spasmodic outboard motor") and because of the ruthless sun "blotted like unspoken anger / behind a casual mist." When the speaker says, "*Your* fore-arms can get scalded, licked with pain," she seems to invite us in—whoever we may be—for exposure to the elements is common. Yet this is not necessarily "authentic" experience, even though the details are there to make it right: the oarlocks, the nets, the outboard motor. We are still following the direction of the *as if,* further reinforced by the hypothetical quality of "*some kind* of sun burning my shoulder blades." We are in a land some-where between the actual and the imaginary—the world of po-etry. To reinforce the mythic element of the experience, Rich interrupts the narrative with a brief, four-line cluster: "The length of daylight / this far north, in this / forty-ninth year of my life / is critical." Now we know more clearly where we are: on a psychic journey at the point in the poet's life where she is feeling her age. Does she have enough daylight to make it safely to shore? Do her remaining years of life seem too short for her to achieve her goal? The poem does not state what that goal is, only that she feels impelled to reach it.

The remainder of this section returns to the narrative of bring-ing the boat to shore, but now we are drawn further in by the beauty of the language: "The glitter of the shoal / depleting into shadow / I recognize: the stand of pines / violet-black really, green in the old postcard." In addition, the mystery intrigues us. The speaker seems to recognize certain features of the land-scape, but we have no clues. Is this someplace where the speaker used to live? Not a new destination but an old one? We must not be too literal about this, and the speaker's commentary reminds us that "Integrity" is a psychic journey: "But really I have noth-ing but myself / to go by." Her tone is calm, almost detached, the rhythms simple and expressive.

Like being in the middle of a dream and knowing you are dreaming, the speaker observes herself, hears herself speak. "Nothing but myself," she repeats. Then she corrects the statement: "My selves. / After so long, this answer." Indeed this poem does have the quality of dream, in this instance, a recurrent one for Adrienne Rich. In section 13 of "Shooting Script," she used the device of being out alone in a boat to convey the sense of her vulnerability in the middle of a journey. In this poem, she writes: "A long time I was simply learning to handle the skiff; I had no special training and my own training was against me." In "Integrity," a journey draws to its close; it is also a return. The second half of the poem brings the rower to the shore and we see what she finds there:

As if I had always known
I steer the boat in, simply.
The motor dying on the pebbles
cicadas taking up the hum
dropped in the silence.
Anger and tenderness: my selves.
And now I can believe they breathe in me
as angels, not polarities.
Anger and tenderness: the spider's genius
to spin and weave in the same action
from her own body, anywhere—
even from a broken web.

The cabin in the stand of pines
is still for sale. I know this. Know the print
of the last foot, the hand that slammed and locked that door,
then stopped to wreathe the rain-smashed clematis
back on the trellis
for no one's sake except its own.
I know the chart nailed to the wallboards
the icy kettle squatting on the burner.
The hands that hammered in those nails
emptied that kettle one last time
are these two hands
and they have caught the baby leaping
from between trembling legs

and they have worked the vacuum aspirator
and stroked the sweated temples
and steered the boat here through this hot
misblotted sunlight, critical light
imperceptibly scalding
the skin these hands will also salve.

Once again, the poet returns to the *as if* phrase, the syntactic patterning of her extended hypothesis. The gentleness of the approach—"As if I had always known / I steer the boat in, simply"—matches the gentleness of the speaker's attitude toward herself. She no longer projects the light or anything else as being "critical" of her. Recognizing "the selves" of which she is composed, Rich develops a metaphor, a correlation, to clarify her self-recognition. Her selves, the "anger and tenderness" she mentions, compose her integrity. Not opposites, but "angels," her "anger and tenderness" are as much a part of one another as the spider's spinning and weaving. The cabin, its contents, and its history in relation to the speaker are an expansion of this newly discovered sense of her integrity.

In coming to the cabin, the speaker seems to be returning to something, possibly a former life. The stanza is filled with what the speaker knows about the former inhabitant of the cabin— who was herself—or herselves. Both anger and tenderness enter into this conception. The tenderness is captured in the image of the hand that "stopped to wreathe the rain-smashed clematis" and in the last image: "the skin these hands will also salve." The anger is contained in the action of leaving the cabin: "the hand that slammed and locked that door." Anger has also driven the speaker to return to this place she had put up for sale. To suggest this, Rich comes back to the metaphor of the journey "through this hot, misblotted sunlight," echoing the image in her first stanza of "a sun blotted like unspoken anger." It is difficult to separate the anger from the tenderness, for the images are linked: "critical light / imperceptibly scalding / the skin these hands will also salve."

We come away from "Integrity" feeling the complexity and enormity of the speaker's maturity, the subtlety and beauty of the

poet's skill in handling her poetic materials. The poem also reminds us of the ending of "Transcendental Etude" from her previous book. In the earlier poem, Rich comes to a new understanding and appreciation of womanly art forms and of her own role as
a woman poet. As in *A Wild Patience,* she discovers within herself
both anger and tenderness. The contrasting images of the "broken glass" and the "soft leaf" compose the "Integrity" of the poet
who knows herself more deeply now than ever as a poet and as a
woman.

Written a year later than "Integrity," the poem "Transit" also
treats the path the poet has taken and the theme of aging, which
is complicated by a sense of physical debilitation. It is a "self-
portrait at fifty," with a speaker who refers to herself as a *cripple*
(Rich has rheumatoid arthritis and walks with a cane). She nar-
rates an encounter with a skier the same age as she, but robustly
healthy:

> When I meet the skier she is always
> walking, skis and poles shouldered, toward the mountain
> free-swinging in worn boots
> over the path new-sifted with fresh snow
> her greying dark hair almost hidden by
> a cap of many colors
> her fifty-year-old, strong, impatient body
> dressed for cold and speed
> her eyes level with mine

This poem turns a psychic event—coming to grips with one's
limitations, one's mortality—into a physical event—an encounter with a fifty-year-old, vigorous skier. We are plunged into the
physical event at the beginning of the poem and do not know
until the line "as she, who I might have been" that the encounter
never actually occurred. But suppose it were possible to meet the
self one might have grown into? While the poem still employs
the self of the poet and is indeed almost brutally naked, it is not
limited by the exigencies of personal expression: authenticity
and sincerity. The "authentic" emerges in fidelity to accurate detail: "the path new-sifted with fresh snow / her greying dark

hair." Sincerity emerges where it counts—in the gradations of Rich's tone.

At first the narrator admires the vigor of the skier: "free-swinging in worn boots" with her "strong, impatient body / dressed for cold and speed." This admiration turns into a touch of envy, maybe even regret: "she passes me as I shall never pass her / in this life." The speaker is physically outclassed and there is nothing she can do about it. "In this life" might seem like a throwaway line, a thought tacked on, but it is not. It is a gauntlet thrown down for a life in which physical eminence has not been an important goal. She might have gone that path. The third stanza revels in nostalgia for a former life of vigorous, physical activity: "climbing Chocorua" with the skier, "summer nine-teen-forty-five." This intense moment in the beauty of the mountain environment seemed "like dreams of flying" when there were, one gathers, no perceived obstacles. Memories like this "haunt" the speaker as she thinks of the split between her present self and her former self. The tone gets somber and speculative as we are asked to imagine whether it might not be the speaker who haunts the skier: "or is it I who do the haunting." Instead of self-denigration or regret, the "supposing" of the poem allows the speaker to develop an alternative insight, equally "authentic" since the encounter occurs in the imagination. This insight is critical of the skier: "how unaware she is / how simple / this is for her." Ending the poem with a question— "the skier / and the cripple must decide / to recognize each other?"—Rich reinforces its hypothetical quality.

If the skier were to recognize the more "soulful" speaker, the "cripple" who gazes in admiration of her vigor, the skier would marry her physicality to a strength of soul. As Rich has written elsewhere, she views woman's "physicality as a resource, rather than a destiny," and that women "must touch the unity and res-onance of our physicality" as "the "corporeal ground of our in-telligence" (*On Lies, Secrets, and Silence*, p. 21). Over the course of her life's work, Rich has been developing an aesthetic of wom-anly power, one aspect of which is a focus upon woman's body as a metaphor of the life-force itself. In "Transit," her focus on the robust physicality of the skier provides us with a more complex sense of that metaphor. Here, the skier is seen as primarily physical, but her woman's body is devoted to a vigorous independence, not to "the passion to make and make again" as Rich writes in her poem "Natural Resources." Giving birth to oneself and others is not the skier's intent. Solitary and independent, she evokes admiration, reminding us of women athletes in the Olympics and elsewhere who have broken through all the masculinist stereotypes of feminine weakness and fragility. Physicality, however, is not enough. The skier's recognition of the speaker's spiritual strength would effect the kind of integration that Rich envisions. The poem, as an act of the mind, models that imagined integration from the speaker's perspective. Since the skier is so "unaware," Rich renders her integration as hypothetical.

The poem's metaphorical terms and conclusions transcend the "real" while deeply partaking of the self of the poet. Employing the strategy of an extended hypothesis, Rich invites us to suppose that an encounter took place with a buried aspect of herself. It is a brilliant rhetorical device. Consistently, when Rich can employ forms that allow this range to her imagination, her poems strike universal chords. The post-modernist mode suits her.

Other poems that are riveted to personal experience are not as evocative as "Integrity" and "Transit." "Rift" is such a poem. It is about an argument a couple has and appears autobiographical:

> I have in my head some images of you:
> your face turned awkwardly from the kiss of greeting
> the sparkle of your eyes in the dark car, driving
> your beautiful fingers reaching for
> a glass of water
>   Also your lip curling
> at what displeases you, the sign of closure,
> the fending-off, the clouding-over.
>   *Politics,*
> you'd say, *is an unworthy name*
> *for what we're after.*

What we're after
is not that clear to me, if politics
is an unworthy name.

When language fails us, when we fail each other
there is no exorcism. The hurt continues. Yes, your scorn
turns up the jet of my anger. Yes, I find you
overweening, obsessed, and even in your genius
narrow-minded—I could list much more—
and absolute loyalty was never in my line
once having left it in my father's house—
but as I go on sorting images of you
my hand trembles, and I try
to train it not to tremble.

Rich captures the agony of the quarrel in the opening list of images: "your face turned awkwardly from the kiss of greeting" and also the finely textured language of "your lips curling / at what displeases you." The center of the poem, the exchange over "Politics," departs from image into statement, but that statement is terse, provocative, and personal to these two people. We feel interested, but excluded—as well we should be, for this is not our quarrel. The challenge of personal expression in poetry, now as always, lies in how to render the universality of the personal. Not everything personal is universal. We all may fight, but not over the same subjects. The "trick" lies in making personal content seem universal. Such "tricks" are the province of the poetic imagination.

In the last section, Rich attempts to bridge the gap between the particular rift that is the subject of her poem and general human problems. The "us" in the first line could be any of us for whom "language fails"; so too the "we" in "when we fail each other." The rest of the poem does not apply to "us" at all. Rooted in a dialogue between the two women, the poem is conversational, its voice authentic and involved. We can imagine her words actually voiced. Because of the nature of this "conversation," metaphor is limited. "Yes, your scorn / turns up the jet of my anger" is the only figurative language. Two particular people quarrel; one is found "overweening, obsessed and . . . narrow-minded." The other has trembling hands. The poem leaves the speaker and us trapped in what actually happened. Without the device of extended hypothesis, Rich narrows her range to personal testimony, a technique that limits the power of her poetry in this volume.

When Rich writes interior monologues, she is more likely to employ the device of extended hypothesis and write "good" poems. Often, when she includes a listener in a dramatic monologue she seems trapped in a shared reality, unable to invent the hypothesis that will free her imagination. Another problem in the dramatic monologues is that the listener, with some minor exceptions, remains a listener. Her characteristic mode is silence and "the deep, difficult troughs" remain "unvoiced." If the listener's silence were broken, the rift might possibly become bridged and the relationship could move to a higher level of intimacy. This problem is an old one for Rich, who appears to possess the power of language more than anyone else she puts into her poems. Since she places such great value on language, in particular the transformation of silence, it must be agony to her not have a partner similarly equipped. Inevitably, the shared, agonized reality of the dramatic monologues maintains its privacy and remains exclusive to the speaker and the listener.

Two poems that appear side by side in the volume will illustrate the difference between the interior monologues and the dramatic monologues. In "What is Possible," a poem of the ruminating self, a woman considers the nature of her own mind. Freed from the necessity of making itself known to one person, this interior monologue asserts a universal significance. "For Memory," a lovely but obscure dramatic monologue, is addressed to someone whom the speaker knows quite well, yet does not know. Another rift appears to exist that the speaker, a gatherer of autumn leaves, is trying to heal. This poem attempts to transcend difference and meet one particular person. Its meanings seem private.

"For Memory" begins with a two-line statement: "Old words: *trust* *fidelity* / Nothing new yet to take their place." Subsequently, the speaker describes her actions in doing the autumn chores and recalling someone's voice "stinging the wires," saying "disloyalty betrayal." Gathering the leaves offers the speaker no surcease from her turmoil over this quarrel. The poem then proceeds to offer a calm solution to their differences:

> I can't know what you know
> unless you tell me
> there are gashes in our understandings
> of this world
> We came together in a common
> fury of direction
> barely mentioning difference
> (what drew our finest hairs
> to fire
> the deep, difficult troughs
> unvoiced)
> I fell through a basement railing
> the first day of school and cut my forehead open—
> did I ever tell you? More than forty years
> and I still remember smelling my own blood
> like the smell of a new schoolbook
>
> And did you ever tell me
> how your mother called you in from play
> and from whom? To what? These atoms filmed by ordinary dust
> that common life we each and all bent out of orbit from
> to which we must return simply to say
> *this is where I came from*
> *this is what I knew*
>
> The past is not a husk   yet change goes on
>
> Freedom. It isn't once, to walk out
> under the Milky Way, feeling the rivers
> of light, the fields of dark—
> freedom is daily, prose-bound, routine
> remembering. Putting together, inch by inch
> the starry worlds. From all the lost collections.

The voice in the poem is gentle in its plea for understanding. Recrimination is hushed: "I can't know what you know / unless you tell me." The poem's rhythms are delicate, for it means to placate and beseech for deeper intimacy with the loved one with whom the speaker "came together in a common / fury of direction / barely mentioning difference." It touches us with the simplicity of its solution and we want to believe that telling "*where I came from / . . . what I knew*" will bridge the "deep, difficult troughs" between them. The intimate "feel" of this poem is amazing. At the end, the tone shifts as Rich tries to leap into a cosmic dimension and to develop a new concept of freedom. She chooses metaphor for her vehicle.

Making a connection between "Freedom" and the kind of memory-probing she asks from her partner, she says it is not a romantic moment under the stars. Why one should feel freedom in such a context is not clarified. The last three lines of the poem seem clear because the syntax is explicit: "freedom is daily, prose-bound, routine / remembering." Yet, no matter how many adjectives pile up, it does not make sense. Stripped and reversed, the statement would go: "remembering is freedom." Only if we remember are we free? Freedom has something to do with creating one's own "starry worlds. From all the lost collections." The language is lovely, the meaning obscure. Perhaps this is a private script between the two people involved. It is not a "common language." To the political prisoner is freedom so obtained? To the poor? This sort of question does not usually arise with Adrienne Rich, who is one of our more politically aware poets. In a poem in which she addresses a particular person about a special aspect of their relationship she becomes insular, the significance of her poem limited.

We encounter a different kind of poem in "What Is Possible." Not constrained by a particular listener, the speaker appears to be musing to herself. As in the previous poem, Rich's imagery comes from the night sky:

> A clear night in which two planets
> seem to clasp each other   in which the earthly grasses
> shift like silk in starlight
>
> If the mind were clear
> and if the mind were simple   you could take this mind
> this particular state   and say

> *This is how I would live if I could choose:*
> *this is what is possible*

The perceptions are beautiful. Simply to see what the poet sees
and to find language for that perception would seem extraordinary to most people whose minds were "clear" and "simple."
However, the rhetorical *ifs* in the poem are followed by *buts* and
the speaker finds it necessary to expand upon her image of the
planets to clarify her meaning:

> A clear night.   But the mind
> of the woman imagining all this   the mind
> that allows all this to be possible
> is not clear as the night
> is never simple   cannot clasp
> its truths as the transiting planets clasp each other
> does not so easily
>   work free from remorse
> does not so easily
>   manage the miracle
> for which mind is famous
>   or used to be famous

As the speaker argues with herself in the process of exploring
her mind she achieves a kind of clarity missing from "For Memory." Curiously, this process of talking with herself generates
more communication and insight than when she establishes a
listener other than herself. Perhaps this is because the poem is
about Rich as a poet and not as a partner in a couple. Speaking
of herself as a poet gives Rich the freedom to be a poet—that is,
to use her imagination to transcend and transform experience.

The last section of "What Is Possible" returns to the *if . . . but*
strategy and articulates, in its finale, a startling, apocalyptic
vision:

> If it could ever come down to anything like
> a comb passing through hair beside a window
> no more than that
>   a sheet
>   thrown back by the sleeper

but the mind
of the woman thinking this   is wrapped in battle
is on another mission
a stalk of grass   dried feathery weed   rooted in snow
in frozen air stirring   a fierce wand graphing

Her finger also tracing
pages of a book
knowing better than the poem she reads
knowing through the poem
                        through the ice-feathered panes
the winter
        flexing its talons
the hawk-wind
          poised to kill

A series of images builds toward the magnificent, if chilling, closure. Through the interplay of these images, the poem creates its own universe and we do not have to look outside it or be a party to a private language in order to understand how the poet develops her meanings. The first two images in this sequence suggest automatic, almost unconscious behavior. In both "a comb passing through" and "a sheet thrown back," Rich emphasizes the mindlessness of the action. In the first, an inanimate object is the actor; in the second, someone sleeping performs a simple reflex. There is no "mind" here, no intelligence operating at full capacity.

The next image cluster is enigmatic, but decipherable. Beginning with "but the mind," Rich gives us a sense of what her "mission" is through the grass image. Creating a winter context with its "snow" and "frozen air," she suggests a climate that is harsh and difficult—the opposite of ease, pleasure, or simplicity. In this climate—let us say the threat of nuclear holocaust during the last quarter of the twentieth century (though this may be going too far; the poem merely suggests)—the poet images her mind as "a fierce wand graphing." The wand of the magician becomes the wand of the poet creating her images, composing her vision as the magician can figure the events of the future.

Connected to the wand image is "her finger also tracing."

Similar in shape to the slim wand, the knowledgeable finger of the poet deciphers a meaning that does not appear in "the poem she reads." The poet is seer, "Knowing better," not just "through the poem" but "through the ice-feathered panes." Thus Rich returns to the climate of winter, the climate of our times, when what she sees ahead is tremendous destruction, a new ice age: "the winter / flexing its talons / the hawk-wind / poised to kill." We accept the poet's vision because facts of contemporary existence confirm it, a fragile balance of powers being all that comes between us and the possibility of nuclear war. Her vision is believable because she has earned it through the materials of her poem and because we can follow the emergence of her understandings. In "What Is Possible," Rich employs traditional poetic devices of metaphor and a cluster of images. She also liberates her imagination with the simple *if . . . but* syntactic pattern, a variation of the extended hypothesis most common to the postmodernist mode.

The problem with the collection is that Rich has included too many poems that do not transcend their occasion. Only a scattering of her poems attain the brilliance of her finest achievements. The final group of poems in *A Wild Patience* illustrates this problem because it includes both the lackluster and the luminous. "Turning the Wheel" is an uneven poem whose weak sections tend to obscure the more effective poetic moments. Sections 6 and 7 of this eight-part poem illustrate why the failings occur, why the success happens.

"Turning the Wheel" is a lengthy poem about a journey to the American Southwest. Sections 1 through 5 describe what the poet found there: "a poor, conquered, bulldozed desert / over-ridden like a hold-out / enemy village." She finds also a "lesbian archeologist" who asks "the clay all questions but her own." The poet cannot "pierce through to a prehistoric culture" nor to the people "known as those who have ceased." In her quest for someone or something still vital, she tries "to imagine a desert-shamaness" but fails: "the shamaness could well have withdrawn her ghost" from this "rich white man's paradise." The Southwest that Rich perceives is bleak. She discovers in it the effects of "colonization," such as the self-hatred of flagellants "in Colcha embroidery." Even so, she maintains her search for something vital. For her, this is "the desert witch, the shamaness." By section 6 we have reached the fine poem "Apparition," in which the shamaness does take form in Rich's imagination:

> If she appears, hands ringed with rings
> you have dreamed about, if on her large fingers
> jasper and sardonyx and agate smoulder
> if she is wearing shawls woven in fire
> and blood, if she is wearing shawls
> of undyed fiber, yellowish
> if on her neck are hung
> obsidian and silver, silver and turquoise
> if she comes skirted like a Christian
> her hair combed back by missionary fingers
> if she sits offering her treasure by the road
> to spare a brother's or an uncle's dignity
> or if she sits pretending
> to weave or grind or do some other thing
> for the appeasement of the ignorant
> if she is the famous potter
> whose name confers honor on certain vessels
> if she is wrist-deep in mud and shawled in dust
> and wholly anonymous
> look at her closely if you dare
> do not assume you know those cheekbones
> or those eye-sockets; or that still-bristling hair.

This poem moves effortlessly between the imaginary and the actual, its rhetorical structure dependent upon the proposition: "If she appears. . . ." Then Rich proceeds to weave together the elements of that appearance, beginning with jewelry and clothing. For centuries, Native Americans wore their wealth in the form of jewelry. Some still do. One often sees women and men at festivals or Indian markets wearing "obsidian and silver, silver and turquoise." We are less likely to see the imaginative "shawls woven in fire / and blood"; more likely to see "shawls of undyed fiber." The effect of the numerous *if* propositions is the creation of an extraordinary portrait that is not one particular woman, but a whole world of shamanesses: one who "sits offering her treasures by the road" as well as "the famous potter / whose name confers honor on certain vessels." Rich's observations of all the types of Native American women she has seen yields a composite portrait. We are warned against thinking we understand what we see if this apparition should appear: "look at her closely, if you dare / do not assume you know those cheekbones / or those eye-sockets; or that still-bristling hair."

Rich's "Apparition" is provocative, her imagery varied and compelling, her rhythms driven by her passionate commitment to the value of women's lives and the enduring mystery of the female principle no matter how "colonized" the land and the people. This poem contains the joy of that mystery in its multitudinous forms, the warning to beware of the fierceness inherent in "that still-bristling hair." Although Rich asserts in her opening poem "The Images" that "no-man's land does not exist," she keeps trying to make one; her deliberate focus upon "lesbian archeologists" and "shamanesses" does not acknowledge the male. Thus she advances her program for poetry. In a poem such as "Apparition," her focus on the female is inspired, helped along by the strategy of extended hypothesis and mythmaking.

In "Mary Jane Colter, 1904," which immediately follows "Apparition," Rich's approach is less inspired, and the poem illustrates some of the weaknesses of this book. Rich adopts the voice of Colter and presents the poem in the form of a letter. In the notes to the volume, Rich explains that "The letter is a poetic fiction, based on a reading of Virginia Grattan, Mary Colter, *Builder upon the Red Earth* (Flagstaff, Arizona: Northland Press, 1980)." Employing an epistolary address, the poem opens:

> My dear Mother and sister:
> I have been asked
> to design a building in the Hopi style
> at the Grand Canyon. As you know
> in all my travels for Mr. Harvey

and the Santa Fe Railroad, I have thought this the greatest
sight in the Southwest—in our land entire.

Whether this poem is "poetic fiction" or not, it does not rise
above its occasion. Rich has used the letter form before, most
notably in "Paula Becker to Clara Westhoff" from her previous
volume *The Dream of a Common Language*. In the earlier poem
she entered the consciousness of Paula Becker, seeming to transform herself into the other woman. She felt what Paula felt,
knew what she knew, dreamed her dreams—or made us imagine
that she did. In "Mary Jane Colter" we get none of that. We get
banalities: "the greatest sight in the Southwest." What feeling
there is, is gentile: "with what elation / this commission has
filled me. I regret to say / it will mean I cannot come home."
Colter's "knowing" is what she projects onto her mother and
sister: "I know my life seems shaky, unreliable / to you." This
poem is superficial and occasional. On the occasion of discovering a woman architect in the Southwest, Rich decided to write
this poem. The lack of passionate involvement shows itself in the
prosy rhythms: "I have been asked / to design a building in the
Hopi style / at the Grand Canyon." Perhaps the artlessness of
these rhythms is deliberate: a letter to one's mother and sister
must seem natural and unaffected. The lack of metaphor may
also be explained in this same fashion. Without passion,
rhythm, striking image, or metaphor, the poem leaves us with
the impression of minor poetic value.

Rich has written from the perspective of a woman architect
before in her 1973 poem "The Fourth Month of the Landscape
Architect." An interior monologue, it renders the consciousness
of the architect with brilliant clarity:

> I touch stylus, T-square, pens
> of immeasurable fineness,
> the hard-edge. I am I,
> this India ink my rain
> which can irrigate gardens, terraces
> dissolve or project horizons
> flowing like lava from the volcano of the inkpot
> at the stirring of my mind.

The difference between the two poems is striking. "Mary Jane Colter, 1904" lacks feeling, imagination, empathy, and vision. "The Fourth Month" is rhythmic, imaginative, metaphorical, in effect, a fine poem.

The problem with "Mary Jane Colter, 1904" is more than the studied artlessness of the letter form. It almost seems as if Rich is willfully pulling away from poetry and its demands. "Apparition" indicates that she still has the power of her poet's skills, but her use of them is arbitrary and undependable.

In 1964, Adrienne Rich told the audience at a poetry reading what the act of writing a poem was like for her: "What I know I know through making poems. Like the novelist who finds that his characters begin to have a life of their own and to demand certain experiences, I find that I can no longer go to write a poem with a neat handful of materials and express those materials according to a prior plan: the poem itself engenders new sensations, new awareness in me as it progresses" (ARP, p. 89). Many of the poems in A Wild Patience no longer give the sense that the poet knows what she knows "through making poems." Competing with the knowledge gained from poems is a prior knowledge of patriarchal evil, "colonization," and the victimization of women—as in a poem like "Frame." Competing also is a commitment to a focus on women and women's concerns and to lesbianism. This specialization leads to poems about Ethel Rosenberg but not Julius, about Willa Cather ("For Julia in Nebraska") because she was a lesbian, for "Mother-in-Law," "Heroines," "Grandmothers." Rich definitely chooses her subjects; one wonders if they ever choose her.

There are signs, however, that this "prior plan" is cracking, to the benefit of Rich's poetry and the well-being of the poet. In the conclusion of the poem "For Ethel Rosenberg," for example, Rich writes:

> if I dare imagine her surviving
> I must be fair to what she must have lived through
> I must allow her to be at last

political in her ways   not in mine
her urgencies perhaps   impervious to mine
defining revolution as she defines it

or, bored to the marrow of her bones
with "politics"
bored with the vast boredom of long pain

small; tiny in fact; in her late sixties
liking her room   her private life
living alone perhaps

no one you could interview
maybe filling a notebook herself
with secrets she has never sold

This conclusion gains its power from the strength of Rich's imagination. That imagination is flexible. As in other poems that succeed in transcending reality, transforming it for the poet and us, Rich employs an extended hypothesis. "If I dare imagine her surviving" provides the starting point. The strength of her imagination allows Rich to project onto Ethel Rosenberg a boredom "to the marrow of her bones / with 'politics.'" What an idea for the "political" Adrienne Rich to admit into her psyche! She admits as well that maybe "the personal" is not "the political" after all, for she imagines that Rosenberg might retreat, "liking her room   her private life." This theme, as a matter of fact, has been an undercurrent in *A Wild Patience* for the poet too would like to repossess a private life and to live in harmony with her partner, "maybe filling a notebook herself / with secrets she has never sold." If all the secrets were out, all the silences broken, there would be no more passion to transform. Rich requires that tension in her poetry, for the power-to-transform silence into speech is a key aspect of her female aesthetic. For silence to occur, the personal or private is essential.

The last section of "Turning the Wheel" reinforces this direction. It carries the same title as the whole poem and describes a road leading to the Grand Canyon and a journey the speaker begins to "the female core / of a continent" but does not complete. She imagines the canyon as "the face / of annihilating and impersonal time / stained in the colors of a woman's genitals / outlasting every transient violation." As in "Integrity," the poet is faced with a sense of her own mortality. That the canyon is female and "strangely intimate" to her does not serve to lessen her fear of it. Contrary to the pattern of "Integrity" where the shore is reached and discoveries made by the solitary traveler, this poem concludes:

> Today I turned the wheel   refused that journey
> I was feeling too alone on the open plateau
> of piñon juniper   world beyond time
> of rockflank spread around me   too alone
> and too filled with you   with whom I talked for hours
> driving up from the desert   though you were far away
> as I talk to you all day   whatever day

In effect, "Turning the Wheel" is a love poem in which the loved one is preferred to any solitary discoveries the poet might make. She is a woman after all and "tender." Although we might have wished for a dramatic confrontation with "annihilating and impersonal time," we get instead an honest expression of genuine feeling. Perhaps there is some guilt on the speaker's part that she "refused that journey." Guilt recedes in her concentration upon her lover who fills her as the scenery cannot. Thus Rich retreats to the personal and the human, away from that canyon which represents for her the abstraction of "impersonal time." Reading this poem we cannot help but feel that this is a genuine discovery for her, a discovery made through the process of writing the poem. Its tone is honest, a combination of fear and sadness. Its rhythms pulse slowly, almost hesitantly to the conclusion that asserts the primacy of feeling and the truths of the human heart.

Since Rich's commitment to feminist beliefs is unstinting, she may well sacrifice the truths of her heart and of poetry for what she perceives as higher purposes: the feminine principle fully integrated into consciousness, society and politics transformed by feminist principles, womanly power recognized and embraced as the key to survival of the human species and life on this planet. "Turning the Wheel," however, may indicate a less sacrificial direction for Adrienne Rich, which is actually an old direction as far as her poetry is concerned. That direction could carry her back to the sources of her poetry, where truths are not preordained but discovered in the process of making the poem.

NOTES

CHAPTER 1. INTRODUCTION

1. *Adrienne Rich's Poetry,* ed. Barbara Charlesworth Gelpi and Albert Gelpi (New York: Norton, 1975), p. xi (hereafter cited as *ARP*).

2. Adrienne Rich, *Sources* (Woodside, Calif.: Heyeck Press, 1983), p. 15.

3. Nancy Milford, "Messages from No Man's Land," review of *A Wild Patience Has Taken Me This Far, New York Times Book Review,* December 20, 1981, p. 21.

4. Robert Dahl, *Modern Political Analysis,* 2d ed. (Englewood Cliffs, N.J.: Prentice-Hall, 1979), pp. 15–16.

5. Elizabeth Janeway, *Powers of the Weak* (New York: Knopf, 1980), p. 3.

6. Dorothy Dinnerstein, *The Mermaid and the Minotaur* (New York: Harper and Row, 1976), p. 60.

7. Adrienne Rich, "The Kingdom of the Fathers," *Partisan Review* 43, no. 1 (Spring 1975): 22.

8. See Sarah B. Pomeroy, *Goddesses, Whores, Wives and Slaves: Women in Classical Antiquity* (New York: Schocken, 1976).

9. Adrienne Rich, *Of Woman Born: Motherhood as Experience and Institution* (New York: Norton, 1976), p. 99.

10. Marija Gimbutas provides extensive anthropological evidence for prehistoric reverence for a female deity in *Goddesses and Gods of Old Europe, 7000–3500 B.C.: Myths, Legends and Cult Images* (Berkeley and Los Angeles: University of California Press, 1982). For a comprehensive survey of the relationship, see Susan Griffin, *Woman and Nature: The Roaring Inside Her* (New York: Harper, 1978). Griffin dedicates her book to Adrienne Rich.

11. Adrienne Rich, "Commencement Address," *Smith Alumnae Quarterly* 70, no. 4 (August 1979): 9.

12. In an introduction to Judy Grahn's poems, Rich connects transformation with women and nature: "When we speak of transformation we speak more accurately out of the vision of a process which will leave neither surfaces nor depths unchanged, which enters society at the most essential level of the subjugation of women and nature by men. We begin to conceive a planet on which both women and nature might coexist as the *She Who* we encounter in Judy Grahn's poems." Rich's introduction is entitled "Power and Danger: Works of a Common Woman (1977)" in her *On Lies, Secrets, and Silence: Selected Prose, 1966–1978* (New York: Norton, 1979), p. 248.

13. Simone de Beauvoir, *The Second Sex*, trans. and ed. H. M. Parshly (New York: Bantam, 1961), pp. 70–71.

14. Rich locates this power in language: "When we become acutely, disturbingly aware of the language we are using and that is using us, we begin to grasp a material resource that women have never before collectively attempted to repossess (though we were its inventors, and though individual writers like Dickinson, Woolf, Stein, H.D., have approached language as transforming power)." *On Lies, Secrets, and Silence*, p. 247.

15. *ARP*, p. xii. Although the Gelpis make a valid and useful distinction between H.D. and Adrienne Rich, H.D. was important to Rich (see note 14 above). Rich also uses as epigraph to *The Dream of a Common Language* a passage from H.D.'s *The Flowering of the Rod*.

16. Karen Horney, *Feminine Psychology* (New York: Norton, 1967), and M. Esther Harding, *Woman's Mysteries* (New York: Pantheon, 1955). For more recent feminist criticism of consciousness, see Annis Pratt, *Archetypal Patterns in Women's Fiction* (Bloomington: Indiana University Press, 1982).

17. Denis de Rougemont, *Love in the Western World*, rev. ed. (1940; rpt. New York: Harper and Row, 1956). Erich Neumann, *The Origins and History of Consciousness* (1949; rpt. Princeton: Princeton University Press, 1970), *Amor and Psyche* (Princeton: Princeton University Press, 1956), and *The Great Mother* (Princeton: Princeton University Press, 1963). Along with de Rougemont and Neumann, Rich cites the work of J. J. Bachofen, Robert Briffault, and Frederick Engels. She states that "though useful as preliminary steps in identifying the phenomenon and in suggesting that the patriarchal family is not an inevitable 'fact of nature,' [their writing] still stops short of recognizing the omnipresence of patriarchal bias as it affects even the categories in which we think, and which has made of even the most educated and

privileged woman an outsider, a nonparticipant, in the molding of culture" (*Of Woman Born,* pp. 39–40).

18. Helen Vendler, "Myths for Mothers," a review of *Of Woman Born, New York Review of Books,* September 30, 1976, p. 17.

19. The issue of a distinctive "female" imagination has come under intense discussion by feminist literary critics. See Patricia Meyer Spacks, *The Female Imagination,* and Ellen Moers, *Literary Women.*

20. Quoted by Ehrich Neumann, *The Origins and History of Consciousness,* p. 376.

21. Terrence Des Pres, "Self/Landscape/Grid," *New England Review/Bread Loaf Quarterly* 5, no. 4 (Summer 1983): 442.

22. Ibid., p. 444. Des Pres's survey took in the current issue of *American Poetry Review, Poetry,* and a random sampling of other magazines. In all, he read more than two hundred poems. The issue in which Des Pres's essay appears, *Writers in the Nuclear Age,* provides overwhelming evidence, however, that Forche and Rich should not be singled out as among the few.

23. Ibid., p. 445.

24. Aaron Kramer, "Hiroshima: a 37-Year Failure to Respond," *New England Review/Bread Loaf Quarterly* 5, no. 4 (Summer 1983): 539.

25. See the preface to the *Poetics of the New American Poetry,* ed. Donald Allen and Warren Tallman (New York: Grove Press, 1973). Allen and Tallman provide an elaboration of the process by which the new critics screened out the Pound and Olson influence from a generation of students.

26. Adrienne Rich, "Letter to the Editor," *Equal Times,* April 15, 1979.

27. Louise Bernikow, "Out of the Bell Jar," *New Times* 7, no. 9 (October 29, 1976): 50.

28. Ibid., p. 51.

29. Ellen Moers, "A Poet's Prose," review of *On Lies, Secrets, and Silence, New York Times Book Review,* April 22, 1979, p. 12.

CHAPTER 2. THE HARDEST THING TO LEARN

1. Elaine Showalter, "Feminist Criticism in the Wilderness," in *Writing and Sexual Difference,* ed. Elizabeth Abel (Chicago: University of Chicago Press, 1982), p. 34.

2. Rich's subversion of the male influence on her poetry is a subject I

deal with more fully in my discussion of her second volume, *The Diamond Cutters*.

CHAPTER 3. THE CAREFUL ARRIVISTE

1. In his review of this volume, Randall Jarrell describes the influence of Frost and Auden. See also Albert Gelpi's "Adrienne Rich: The Poetics of Change" for a description of the influence of Yeats, Stevens, and Eliot (*ARP*, p. 132) W. H. Auden also points out particular influences in his introduction to *A Change of World* (*ARP*, p. 126) Although I choose to concentrate upon one of these influences, a case could be made for the effect of the others.

2. Tillie Olsen, *Silences* (New York: Delacorte Press, 1978), pp. 16–17.

CHAPTER 4. THE SONG OF SILK

1. Virginia Woolf, *Orlando* (New York, 1928), p. 188.

2. Carol Gilligan, *In a Different Voice* (Cambridge: Harvard University Press, 1982), p. 16.

3. Rich writes about the making of "Snapshots" in her essay "When We Dead Awaken": "In the late fifties I was able to write, for the first time, directly about experiencing myself as a woman. The poem was jotted in fragments during children's naps, brief hours in a library, or at 3 A.M. after rising with a wakeful child. I despaired of doing any continuous work at this time. Yet I began to feel that my fragments had a common consciousness and a common theme, one which I would have been very unwilling to put on paper at an earlier time because I had been taught that poetry should be 'universal,' which meant, of course, non-female. Until then I had tried very much not to identify myself as a female poet" (*ARP*, p. 97).

4. In a later gloss on this section, Rich acknowledges her debt to Simone de Beauvoir's *The Second Sex* for some of her images (*ARP*, p. 16). It is quite possible that Rich's reading of this book influenced her in other sections as well.

5. See Patricia Meyer Spacks, *The Female Imagination* (New York: Knopf, 1975), for a discussion of women writers and the use of birds as metaphors for the self.

6. See Harold Bloom, *The Anxiety of Influence: A Theory of Poetry* (New York: Oxford University Press, 1973). Bloom studies, of course, male poets.

CHAPTER 5. MORE THAN A SYMPTOM

1. Tillie Olsen, *Silences* (New York: Delacorte Press, 1978), p. 45.

2. Rich's phrase, "My soul, my helicopter," echoes the last section of "Snapshots" and the image of the emergent woman as a "helicopter, / poised, still coming, / her fine blades making the air wince." In the poem under discussion, the poet appears to have absorbed her own mythology.

3. Virginia Woolf, *A Room of One's Own* (New York: Harcourt, Brace and World, 1929), p. 91.

4. Adrienne Rich, "Vesuvius at Home: The Power of Emily Dickinson," *Parnassus* 5, no. 1 (Fall–Winter 1976): 53.

5. Barbara Grizzuti Harrison, review of Rich's *On Lies, Secrets, and Silence: Selected Prose, 1966–1978, New Republic,* June 2, 1979, p. 36.

6. Rich, "Vesuvius at Home," p. 49.

7. "Tulips" first appeared in the *New Yorker* 38, no. 7 (April 7, 1962): 40, and also in *New Poems,* ed. Lawrence Durrell (New York: Harcourt, Brace and World, 1963), pp. 94–95.

8. Jon Rosenblatt, *Sylvia Plath: The Poetry of Initiation* (Chapel Hill: University of North Carolina Press, 1979), p. 29.

9. Rich, "Vesuvius at Home," p. 64.

CHAPTER 6. NO BETTER POETRY IS WANTED

1. Alicia Ostriker, "In Mind: The Divided Self in Women's Poetry," in *Poetics: Essays on the Art of Poetry,* compiled by Paul Mariani and George Murphy in *Tendril Magazine* 18 (1984): 132.

CHAPTER 7. THE MIND OF THE POET IS CHANGING

1. Charles Olson, "Letter to Elaine Feinstein, May 1959," in *The Poetics of the New American Poetry,* ed. Donald Allen and Warren Tallman (New York: Grove Press, 1973), p. 162.

2. David Kalstone, review of *The Will to Change: Poems, 1968–1970,* in *Reading Adrienne Rich: Reviews and Re-Visions, 1951–1981,* ed. Jane Roberta Cooper (Ann Arbor: University of Michigan Press, 1984), p. 223. Cooper has also included the most comprehensive and extensive bibliography of materials by and about Adrienne Rich.

3. Hugh Kenner, *The Pound Era* (Berkeley and Los Angeles: University of California Press, 1971), p. 146.

4. Susan Sontag, "Eye of the Storm," *New York Review of Books,* February 21, 1980, p. 38.

CHAPTER 8. THE TRAGEDY OF SEX

1. See also Susan Griffin, *Woman and Nature: The Roaring Inside Her* (New York: Harper, 1978). In her review of Griffin's book, Rich says that it is about "female anger as power, female presence as transforming force" (quoted on the back cover of *Woman and Nature*). These themes are also present in *Diving into the Wreck* and *The Dream of a Common Language.*

2. *ARP,* p. 98. Rich has changed this paragraph in a more recent publication of this essay. By 1976, she has given up trying to talk with men: "To the eye of a feminist, the work of western male poets now writing reveals a deep, fatalistic pessimism as to the possibilities of change, whether societal or personal, along with a familiar and threadbare use of women (and nature) as redemptive on the one hand, threatening on the other; and a new tide of phallocentric sadism and overt woman-hating which matches the sexual brutality of recent films. 'Political' poetry by men remains stranded amid the struggles for power among male groups; in condemning U.S. imperialism or the Chilean junta the poet can claim to speak for the oppressed while remaining, as male, part of a system of sexual oppression. The enemy is always outside the self, the struggle somewhere else. The mood of isolation, self-pity, and self-imitation that pervades 'non-political' poetry suggests that a profound change in masculine consciousness will have to precede any new male poetic—or other—inspiration. The creative energy of patriarchy is fast running out; what remains is its self-generating energy for destruction. As women, we have our work cut out for us" (*American Poets in 1976,* ed. William Heyen [Indianapolis: Bobbs-Merrill, 1976], p. 292).

3. Adrienne Rich, *Sources* (Woodside, Calif.: Heyeck Press, 1983), p. 15.

CHAPTER 9. A WHOLE NEW POETRY

1. Willi Appel, *Harvard Dictionary of Music* (Cambridge: Harvard University Press, 1944 and 1969), p. 307.

2. Gertrude Stein, *Lectures in America* (New York: Vintage, 1975), p. 231.

3. Ibid., p. 233.

4. Mary Daly, *Gyn/Ecology: The Metaethics of Radical Feminism* (Boston: Beacon Press, 1978).

CHAPTER 10. THE FEMALE CORE

1. Louis Zukofsky, "A Statement for Poetry," in *The Poetics of the New American Poetry*, ed. Donald Allen and Warren Tallman (New York: Grove Press, 1973), p. 143.
2. Jonathan Holden, *The Rhetoric of the Contemporary Lyric* (Bloomington: Indiana University Press, 1980), p. 136.